Celtic Ways to Pray

CELTIC WAYS TO PRAY

FINDING GOD IN THE NATURAL ELEMENTS

RUTH LINDBERG PATTISON

Morehouse Publishing
NEW YORK

Morehouse Publishing, 19 East 34th Street, New York, NY 10016
Morehouse Publishing is an imprint of Church Publishing Incorporated.

Cover design by Dylan Marcus McConnell, Tiny Little Hammers
Typeset by Denise Hoff

Library of Congress Cataloging-in-Publication Data

Names: Pattison, Ruth Lindberg, author.
Title: Celtic ways to pray : finding God in the natural elements / Ruth
    Lindberg Pattison.
Description: New York, NY : Morehouse Publishing, [2022]
Identifiers: LCCN 2021046723 (print) | LCCN 2021046724 (ebook) | ISBN
    9781640654303 (paperback) | ISBN 9781640654310 (ebook)
Subjects: LCSH: Spiritual life--Celtic Church. | Prayer--Celtic Church. |
    Spirituality--Celtic Church.
Classification: LCC BR748 .P38 2022 (print) | LCC BR748 (ebook) | DDC
    248.089/916--dc23/eng/20211005
LC record available at https://lccn.loc.gov/2021046723
LC ebook record available at https://lccn.loc.gov/2021046724

CONTENTS

INTRODUCTION

About My Theological Journey

I sat on the couch in the living room. Alone. Hands at my sides, palms up, the rough red sculpted upholstery of the 1950s era pleasing against the back of my hands. I thought to myself, "If I could just never sin again, I would be clean forever." I was eight years old.

I had been baptized that day at Riverview Baptist Church in McKeesport, Pennsylvania. Both of my parents had been brought up there, but we attended Grace Baptist across town near our house, our own neighborhood church that we could walk to on Sunday mornings.

A white cotton choir robe, bare feet, and three steps down into the pool of water. My sister helped me choose a Bible verse to recite from the pool for the congregation to hear. Our selection was based solely on brevity because I had to say it by heart. It was the shortest possible verse we could find. Romans 3:23, "All have sinned and fall short of the glory of God." Hers was slightly longer. She was three years older and more adept at memorization. "For the wages of sin is death, but the free gift of God is eternal life. . . ." Same book, sixth chapter, twenty-third verse.

The pastor's right arm was behind my neck and shoulders, his left hand held a white folded handkerchief over my nose and mouth, and three quick dips backward. One for the Father. One for the Son. One for the Holy Ghost. I noticed that the inside of the handkerchief didn't actually get wet. I could still smell the ironing. And miraculously, I could still breathe.

My childlike faith in Jesus, the only Son of God, who died for our sins. In the sense that he died for me, I could be forgiven, and trade in my guilt and sin-sick soul for the blood of the Lamb that would wash me clean. A soul washed clean by the blood of the Lamb. I wanted that. I loved Jesus, plus I didn't want to go to hell. That was the penalty. For Sin. And they said Jesus paid the price. I guessed that's what Paul meant by "wages."

The theological word for this notion is the Atonement, or as I have renamed it for myself: The Cosmic Swap. This is the theological idea that there is an exchange, him for me, price and wage, penalty and payment.

Paul writes things besides our memory verses in the Letter to the Romans. He writes that ever since the creation of the world God's invisible nature, namely God's power and deity, has been revealed in the things that have been made. God revealed. God known. God created heaven, and earth, and makes God's self known, through creation. I like that idea better than the part about sin and its wages. God in the things that have been made. To think that we can know God that way, through the material of the created world, and be saved by it.

How is it that we know something? Epistemology is a branch of philosophy that considers the origin, nature, methods, and limits of human knowledge. Spirituality asks the epistemological question: How is it that we know God? I can know God the same way I know the rough red sculpted upholstery on the skin of the back of my hand. And know salvation. Water, earth, air, and fire—or you, and me, and all the other stuff that has been made. God bearers. God revealers. We can know God in the body.

The catechism, an "Outline of the Faith" in the Episcopal Book of Common Prayer, says that our ritual sacraments are "patterns of countless ways God uses material things to reach out to us."[1] Material things. All matter has the potential to bring God. God uses material things to reach out to us. I want that—to be reached by God. That's why I go outside. God is in the elements, and God is looking for me, and I want to be found. Salvation is out there, in the world, in creation.

Soteriology is the study of the saving work of Christ, and we might say it asks the epistemological question, "How is it that we know that are we saved?" One traditional way of answering that is to talk about the Atonement, the Cosmic Swap, and say that we are saved through the death and resurrection of Jesus Christ. By the blood of the Lamb and the exchange, him for me, price and wage, penalty and payment.

Although Christ's death on the cross is essential to his work as the Son of God, it is not, for me, the singular work by which we are saved, or forgiven of our sins, or reconciled, or through which we know God. I rather think that his death was a necessary feature of real incarnation—a result, and consequence, of his being human. I am saved by the saving acts of God, all of them: God's act of creating, God's act of becoming human, and God's act of dying, and rising from the dead.

The author of the Gospel according to John writes about Jesus in this way: "In the beginning was the Word and the Word was with God and the Word was God" (John 1:1), and "without him, there was not anything made, that was made" (cf. John 1:3), and "The Word became flesh and dwelt among us" (John 1:14). You remember it from midnight mass on Christmas Eve. God, born of a woman, in manger hay, and human family. Incarnation. God with a body. Flesh. Earth and substance. Matter. God using material things to reach out to us, "from heaven to earth come down," God in human form. God, in a body. For us to know.

Jesus is the Incarnate Person of the Trinity and his work fits into a larger arc, a sweeping magnum opus that begins in the act of Creation. "Without him not one thing came into being" (John 1:3). He is God in human form, becoming one with his creation to reach out and find God's humanity from within God's humanity. It is as much in his creating and in his becoming human that I am saved, found, kept, and loved. For me, his death and resurrection are more about Divine Love becoming human, and the healing and consecrating of the human body, and his calling us out of the hiding that we began in Eden, than they are about the theology of Atonement. Christ's death, and resurrection, are of a piece with the act of Creation.

The theology of the Incarnation suggests that we know God through the body. God taking the form of a human being hallows all humanity. Like Mary, all flesh holds the potential to bear God, every face reveals the face of Christ, and every baptism is a nativity: a bursting of holy water, and a birthing of the Divine. God in human form, and the physical world of matter, bears God; all flesh is holy. Incarnation is at the core of my spirituality, and is the motivation, and inspiration, for my priesthood. God is revealed in human existence, and is known in human experience.

The Creation sings a song, and we number it among the Canticles in the morning rite of Daily Prayer: "Omnia Opera Domini." All the world, sing to the Lord.[2] The church thinks it is worth beginning our day that way, every day, everyone, everywhere: to position ourselves, ground our being, locate our existence in the created order, and join in. Praying creation and creation praying. Singing it. Praying the elements of creation because God is in them.

The world becomes our oratory, and prayer becomes our orienteering, our compass work. Finding our way. Where am I, and where is God? God is in the elements, and God uses material things to reach out to us. That's why I go outside. To find and be found.

From any given point of the compass rose, direction is always toward God. If I go north, God is in the earth; if I go south, God is in the fire; if I go east, God is in the air and wind; and if I go west, God is in the water. I cannot go beyond God's reach. Every footfall, a pilgrimage. Every breath, a chanting psalm. Every eye opening, an enlightenment. Every bathing, the font of my being. This God uses material things to reach out to us. This God, who gathers the wind in God's fists (Psalm 104:4), calms a storm on the sea and walks on water (Mark 4:39 and Matthew 14:25), who rides the wind like a chariot, and wraps himself in light as with a garment (Psalm 104), and who scoops up mud to shape a man (Genesis 2:7), this is an elemental God. This God who plays with Leviathan (Psalm 104:26), and draws the circumference of the great deep (Proverbs 8:27); this God who speaks from a bush that burns and says, "'Moses, Moses! . . . Remove the sandals from your feet, for the place on which you are standing is holy ground'" (Exodus 3:4), this is an elemental God. Holy ground. Hallowed. Because God is in it. The whole creation sings.

As a parish priest, I see my daily work as an extension of baptism and Eucharist, inviting people to more than the seven sacraments listed in the prayer book, a sacramental life, finding God in the matter of their daily lives and partnering with them in a life of meaning-making. As preacher, and celebrant, I point to, and lift up, the material substance of their lives, and proclaim that God reveals the sacred out of the mundane; the physical is spiritual; and that matter is holy. And, as a priest, I bless it, which is to say that it is good, and that God is in it, just as I do with the bread and wine at Holy Eucharist and with water at baptism. Every table a holy feast, and every bread broken the body of Christ, every face washed a reflection of the beloved waking. God is in the daily life. So, the life is holy. I preach the elements. I bless the elements. I pray the elements and sing them. Because God is in them.

So, Creation, Salvation, Epistemology, Soteriology, Revelation, Incarnation, Crucifixion, Resurrection? Long story short: We can know God through the body. Our own, and God's. We can find God in matter. And we can be saved.

About the Initiatives for Prayer

If you are an adventurer at heart, consider the initiatives to be a form of spiritual play. If you're the scientific sort, consider them a form of spiritual research, and experiment. Or, if you're the curious detective type who loves a mystery and wants to discover something, approach the directives as spiritual investigation. Think of them as a workbook, or a "how-to" manual, if you're the kind of person who likes a project. Give yourself room to make it your own.

The "Initiatives for Prayer" portion of each chapter is my invitation to you to experiment with prayer, which for the purpose of this book is the process of finding God in the elements. Try some of the ideas in this activity part of the book if you would like, and keep it light-hearted and open-ended. Approach it with a try-it-and-see attitude that invites freedom and the opportunity for discovery.

I have drawn some of the initiatives from my own personal practices, experiments I have conducted for my own spiritual interest. Some I have designed in my work with adult spiritual formation, or for use with retreat groups. So, you might want to try the initiatives on your own, but you might have fun trying some with a partner or using them to enliven conversation with a book group. You could even use them to lead others on a retreat.

The ideas are designed as a practical prayerful engagement of the theological tenets of Creation, Incarnation, and Resurrection. The purpose is to help us see, hear, taste, touch, and smell God. To help us name. To heighten our holy awareness. To fully engage our whole being in the experience of God. The initiatives are there for you to use if you want. Pick and choose, try some and skip some. Approach it like a cookbook because everyone has his or her own tastes.

The prayer initiatives in this book are invitations. We will experiment with body prayer. Listening. Finding words. Making gestures. Playing with things for prayer. We will strike flint and make fire, reach into mud, breathe in deep and blow out, and splash water to find God. Not every prayer initiative will produce the God-moment you've always been waiting for, or the result, or an I-have-arrived kind of moment. They are simply hands-on ways to pray this journey of finding God in the body, in the elements, in the material substance of creation, which is a lifelong process. This book comes alongside you in your spiritual journey for this brief window of, and occasion for, exchange and engagement.

Thank you for the opportunity to journey with you.

A How-to for the Oratory and the Prayer Journal

Let me describe the two items I mention frequently in these prayer initiatives. One is an oratory. The other is a prayer journal.

The Oratory

The oratory is a little more nuanced, so let's begin there. The idea of an oratory is to give voice to, or to pray. Earth, air, water, and fire function like cardinal directions on a compass for finding God. They deliver God to us, in substance. In this book you will see that my practice of prayer is to go outside, to immerse myself in the elements because God is in them, or to bring the elements in, whichever the case may be. The turned spigot at the pedestal sink brings water, and with it, a gully-washing moment of God in the house.

In some parishes, an associate priest with a feverish want to pray and to teach other people to pray finds a space, a corner, an old storage closet, a throughway or passage, and turns it, with gold paint and deep, flat blue paint, like the heavens or Mary's vestment, along with a rack of votive candles, into an oratory. And people go to pray.

An oratory is a place of prayer. It is usually a tiny little room with tapers, and votives, and perhaps icons, in close proximity to the space for corporate worship and the gathered community. But literally, "oratory" means "to give voice to." Ora. Oral. Oratory. Giving voice.

This book is an oratory of sorts. My giving voice and praying with my body. It is my act of melting wax, and holy flame, and throwing myself to the pavement in a gesture of body prayer. Lying prostrate. Vesting for Holy Eucharist, and standing at the altar lifting up bread and wine and blue, gesturing with what we call the orans position, gives voice with my body to the human want for the divine. Standing on holy ground, and dishing out sacred food, and calling it bread from heaven. Pavement. Marble and ancient plank. We lay ourselves down.

For the prayer initiatives described in each chapter, you will need to construct a portable, travel-ready, carry-around, Johnny-on-the-spot oratory, if you would like to use one with this book. Make, find, or buy the container that will become your prayer-on-the-hoof oratory, and mark it in some way with the compass rose, because the essential quest is to find God in the elements at every compass point, in every direction. You might just draw the compass rose on a piece of paper and place it inside of your container.

The most basic approach could be to get a brown paper lunch bag from the pantry. Other options: a tin tea box from the grocery store emptied of its tea, a shoe box, a cigar box, a jewelry box, an oatmeal cardboard tube, a jar with a lid, a container of your choosing that you could imagine becoming a holy container of treasure. In this portable oratory you might place a few things that I suggest, but mostly, your own inspiration will lead you to add treasures along the way. Just the other day, as I dashed to my car and off to work, I found a gray bird feather with a single white stripe down the middle. A treasure. Three days earlier, my grown boy brought me a tiny bird's nest that he found face down in the woods. Moments of breathless knowing that God's spirit is wind, God's body, wing. And my day, perched, and ready.

Earth, fire, water, and air are the compass points for finding God, and all the world our oratory. An oratory is our place of prayer, whether it takes the form of the human body or a room, a tea tin, or the whole wide earth.

The Prayer Journal

In general, journal-keeping is a well-worn spiritual practice and is widely understood as writing something down. The same applies here. Finding a simple bound booklet of paper and whatever kind of writing utensil you like best will suffice.

The booklet can be stapled sheets of plain paper, a spiral college-ruled notebook, a composition book like the ones we all used in third grade, or something a little chicer like a Moleskin. Then choose your favorite tool: freshly sharpened pencils accompanied by a pink pearl block eraser, a bona fide fountain pen with ink jar and nib, a selection of colored felt tips—suit your fancy.

On some occasions I will offer initiatives for the prayer journal that move you through a process of guided steps, or some kind of practice and procedure. On other occasions I will simply suggest you write down your thoughts or reflections and discoveries. You may want to use your journal in a myriad of other ways, so you can work out your own theology with jot and tittle.

Often I will recommend writing a prayer in your journal. So, this is one easy ready reference if you need a place to start: with a collect, the name of which is pronounced with the accent on the first syllable. For a simple prayer form, the collect is a three-part prayer.

A. The Address. "Dear God." This is where you decide what name, or role, or function you want to use for God. Many collects start out with the words, "O God, who . . ."

B. The Request. This is related linguistically to the name you decided to use in the address. It is focused and descriptive, not a laundry-list kind of moment.

C. "In Your Name We Pray." This may be a reconnection, and perhaps an elaboration, on parts A and B.

Additionally, in this modern age of electronic tools some might prefer a keyboard for writing. If you do, then use one. The smart phone offers a lovely journaling component with the ever-ready camera lens, a very rich way to enhance the journaling experience. The phone may also provide a convenient and spontaneous way to list things by using the notepad icon or dictating with the microphone button as a way of capturing thoughts on the ready and composition on the fly.

Anything goes if it will make the prayer journal work for you. It is your journal, after all. Your choice. Your design. Your adventure with prayer.

PART I

God in Earth

To include rock, stone, ash, clay, cliff,
crevice, mud, soil, mineral, decaying
matter, soot, humus, and loam.

We come from God, unearthed from divine substance, our beginnings from the foundations of the world. Cretaceous. Jurassic, Triassic, Paleozoic. "You that seek the Lord. Look to the rock from which you were hewn" (Isaiah 51:1). Creator is sculptor and stone. You, hewn out of rock, out of God. Humanity birthed from a quarry. Born of divine rock. Dug from God. Chiseled stone from stone. An excavation of the Sacred One. Sameness. Bone of bone. Verity.

Earth is sacred matter. Earth delivers God in human form. Rock. Mud. Stone. Unsophisticated, uncomplicated. Primitive. Ancient. Elemental, like God. Adam, like God. Adam of clay, a terracotta compound in God's hand. Mud for fashioning. A likeness of divine image. Same substance. Holy substance.

Our accommodations were four- and five-star hotels. The kind that remove us from the earthier side of the lands we travel. You know, the ones with full-service spas that outfit us with mud masks, lava rubs, sea salt baths, and complimentary potions and lotions concocted from fruits, and herbs, and oils from the musk deer.

But then we arrived in the Old City of Jerusalem itself. To my extreme pleasure, we stayed in the hostel at Christ Church, Jerusalem, where even the floors made my heart leap with the warmth of stone every time I opened the door to my room. Delicate striated color, hard, unmoving, and muffled underfoot, and deeply welcoming. Like coming home.

As it turned out, the construction codes for Jerusalem provided for but one building material, that of native rock. Essential rock, to preserve the ancient youth and beauty of Jerusalem the Golden. Approaching from the west at sunset, I saw that the entire city glistened and gleamed golden, on fire with light and life. The City of God. Itself a testament in stone to God's glory. The beauty of Zion, Jerusalem, "my holy hill" (Psalm 2:6).

The ancient poets and prophets who penned our Holy Scriptures understood God as rock. "He alone is my rock and my salvation, my fortress; I shall never be shaken" (Psalm 62:2). God is a stronghold, a crag, and haven. "The Lord is my rock, my fortress, and my deliverer, my God, my rock in whom I take refuge, my shield, and the horn of my salvation, my stronghold" (Psalm 18:2). "You are a hiding place for me; you preserve me from trouble" (Psalm 32:7a). "But the Lord has become my stronghold, and my God the rock of my refuge" (Psalm 94:22). God as unhewn rock, "the quarry from which you were dug" (Isaiah 51:1).

The image of God as rock is primitive and harkens to a spirituality that evokes our primitive existence, even our preverbal and precognitive experience. A spiritual wisdom, not learned but inborn, of our being and of our bodies. God as rock is spiritual substance and source for our most fundamental human needs: our need for safety, security, shelter, and the ability to trust.

The spirituality of knowing God as rock is not so concerned with such things as the authority, theology, and tradition of the church as it is with our sense of security, based in being and belonging. The infant experience. The satisfaction of rest in God. Body suspended in the strength of God's being. Rocked and cradled. Prayer becomes a positioning; we position ourselves in God. Instead of knowing God as a personality, we know God as place. We know God as substance.

Religion is concerned with rules, and orthodoxy, and right prayer. God as earth is, instead, elemental and, in contrast, begs a spirituality that is all about safety and shelter. Waiting in God. Resting in God. Existing in God. Like the experience of running from danger, finding a crevice in a rock mountain for safety, silencing your breath, heart pounding in your ears. Like the childhood game of hide-and-seek. Prayer without words. It is a positioning. Instead of the mighty saving acts of God, we discover that God is, in and of God's own self, safety: stationary, strong, and steadfast by God's very being.

This sort of spirituality is not as likely to make a statement of faith or think through the rationales of a creed as it is to trust. Instead of conversation, we meet God as silent and learn a nonverbal way of being. Our full body weight released into the substance and strength of God in a passionate experience like that encountered by lovers. Enfolded. Lost as a rock in a quarry, where both rock and quarry are indistinguishable. Weight. Substance. Immovable. Center-of-the-universe trust.

Earth and rock are how the ancients knew God, how they found God. Earth and rock are how I find God. The ancient Celts lived close to the earth, in the immediacy of and the exposure to the elements, and found

God to be just as immediate and fresh. God in the wind in your hair, or the rain on your back, and in the earth underfoot. God was fully present in the physical life without the confines or authority of rules, orthodoxy, and right prayer. Also, the British Isles were geographically removed from the church as empire, absolving Celtic spirituality of the need for conformity and institutional demand.

The high sacramental theology of the church, if there is such, is that the institutionalized practice of sacrament is a nod in the direction of an unbounded experience of a beautiful, unspoiled truth of God in the elements. The institutional church offers a pattern; Celtic spirituality is the thing itself—the life lived. God is present in the elements, and all creation serves as theophany. The Celts simply lived it, celebrated it, sang it, prayed it, and laid down to rest in it. They weren't afraid to touch it, declare it for themselves, to handle it with jovial care in the smooring of the fire, or the baking of the bread, or the milking of the cow.

A central thread of Celtic spirituality is that all of creation was brought into being out of God's being rather than, as the theological notion of *ex nihilo* suggests, out of nothing. The act of creation was God bringing something out of the very substance and existence of God. It follows that all of creation is a theophany. All of creation has the potential to reveal God to us. Creation itself is sacred: a God-bearer. At the center of everything is the light that darkness has not overcome. The life of all things is God's beating heart at the center of every created thing.

A particular, lovely, dramatic truth from story: John, the beloved disciple who penned our gospel, sat next to Jesus at the Last Supper. Actually, they reclined, as they would have in first-century culture. John writes that he reclined next to Jesus and leaned in close enough to speak in whispers about something that was troubling him. From that lean-in to Jesus's chest, John would have been able to hear his heart beating. From this vignette, Celtic spirituality coined the phrase "listening for the heartbeat of God."[3] In this Incarnate One, whom we call Jesus, God's heart beats. Celtic spirituality holds dear the practice of listening for that heartbeat of God in all of creation.

As a priest in the Episcopal Church, I am keenly aware that the church does not own, control, or negotiate a person's ability to find or be found by God. The church simply offers sacrament, which is our way of lifting up the elements—of bread and wine, for example—and saying that God is in them. A sacramental life is the one we live when we leave, out through the church doors, knowing that God is in our bellies, and is in fact in all bread broken. Every table or bundled knapsack of bread is a divine feast worth celebrating because God is in the bread, in all bread. Because God is present in the earth, and grain, and sun, and rain that brought the bread to the table. We can find God there.

The catechism says that the sacraments are "patterns."[4] I am a seamstress, so to me, the word "pattern" is exciting. It means I can take that pattern and make something of my own. Something that fits me particularly, something that I can actually wear, that I can live inside of, that makes me ready to go out into the world to find God. Sacrament as pattern empowers me to put it to use, to live a holy sacramental life that emanates God. The pattern of breaking bread at the eucharistic table gives us a way to see and find God in any bread broken—in the bread I break with my children, or with an aging friend, or in sharing a sandwich with a beggar on the street, and knowing that we are in communion, one body, with one another, and with the Christ.

The catechism also says that God "does not limit himself" to the sacramental rites of the church, but that there are "countless ways by which God uses material things to reach out to us."[5]

Material things. The world of matter. God uses matter to reach out to us, and we can find God in matter. So, I can go outside, and hold up a handful of loam or humus, and say "God is in this earth," or I can lift up an infant human form over a font and say, "God is in this child." God is in the matter. Physical and spiritual are inextricably bound together. The sacraments are reminders to live it and look for it. We remember together in community that the spiritual realities of life are manifest in the physical world, and that our own individual lives are full of God. The sea-breeze on the coast of Ireland smells of a salty deity; the green hills offer a gentle earthy bedding with the sacred for the four-footed and wooly, or for the two-footed walking upright with a staff. We are matter, and we find and meet God in that matter, in our bodies. We are walking, talking, heart-beating sacrament. We are matter, material substance, through which God reaches out to us, and we are tangled up with God in our very own being.

Our first images of God are in the faces of mothers and fathers who bring us into the world, and who nurture us in our earliest moments, and carry us on our way to health, and wholeness, or not. But they are interchangeable, God and mother, God and father, not just because of the parent-child relationship, but because we, all our physical stuff of matter, are infused with the divine, and so we are the face of God for one another. God in human form: God in my human form, and in your human form, as in the human form of the Incarnate One. Formed of the dust.

Creation itself is an expression of God's being, something out of God's own substance, and humanity a more particular expression of God's image. Life is saturated with God, the physical permeated with the spiritual, and the spiritual dependent on the physical to be manifest. This is why, as a priest, I know that if I have disappointed a parishioner, their disappointment is with God. This is why, as a mother, if my children are angry with me, they are angry with God. This is why, as a wife, if I am swept up in the ecstatic love of my beloved, I am swept up with God.

Therein lie the thrill and the risk. If it is all God, reaching out to us through matter, then God is at our fingertips, and in our touching, God is in the scent of a petunia, in my daydreaming on the porch swing, or my snatching a conch shell out of its tumbling in the surf. God is present to me in all of it, and yet it is not idyllic. The risk is enormous, and equally weighty, with the Divine. The possibility for damage and destruction, profound.

A mother exasperated and exhausted with the immediacy of a three-year-old underfoot in the kitchen, hissed and yanked his arm: "Stephen. I don't need a shadow." Whether we want it or not, we are God's image. For that fragile moment, would that it were not so. Had some God image in her life pushed her away, wounded her with such an unbearable rejection that she, for her own self, lost God, and all want for holy intimacy? Did she never know God's want for her to follow God around so closely as to be underfoot, in God's shadow, or hiding under God's wing? She could not see her child as a God image enticing her back into the playful shadow dance of devotion. For that one day in the kitchen, she could not name herself to be a God image, and offer her toddler divine shelter and hiding place, and make it "a God-reached moment" for her little boy. Who among us has not dissolved in the guilt and sorrow of our God-defying behavior, and regretted the wreckage in our wake? We cannot always come through, and so we explore other holy possibilities like confession, and absolution, the freedom of forgiveness, and the rite of reconciliation, and all manner of repair. All of these are healing salve, and give us the chance to see death through to its completion, which is to say, to resurrection.

The elemental God. God as earth. Substance. Rock and stone. Forest floor. Humus. Clay and cliff. Ash and soot. Quarry. We are of God. The earth as holy expression and divine manifestation. The earth is sacred, and we are of the earth. Human. Incarnate. God in form and substance. We mine the earth for mud mask, and lava rub, for the spa life, and being born again. Feet on the ground. Knowing as we are known.

> Throughout history stone has always carried a religious significance and the Celtic peoples recognized this as they took something vitally important in the pre-Christian world and brought it into the new world of Christianity. When they placed these standing stone crosses so prominently in the landscape, they were saying something about the place of the cross in their lives. Here, in the words of Patrick Thomas, is "Celtic Christian stonework with the message of creation restored and made whole by the cross of Christ."[6]

In earth and stone, we find return to God, and the peace and pleasure of coming home. Earth to earth. Ashes to ashes. Dust to dust. The divine matter of which we are made.

1

WHAT DOES GOD SMELL LIKE?

My brother says he can remember how she smells. Our mother. I've always thought him a mystic for it. That's what five years and birth order will do for you—make you a mystic, on top of being a genius. But it's because of the earth. We all smell of earth. God birthed the earth, and then scooped some up to fashion Adam, which is to say: me, you, her. My mother, whom my brother can still remember in a scent. She died when he was eight years old. I was three.

Earth smells of God. And we smell of earth. Humus. Human. Drafting the scent of the Divine. Swirls of God-filled air, like perfume when someone has already left the room. His smelling her is his smelling God. My missing her is my missing God. My anger, my sadness, my joy, and my bliss are all about God. My thrill at the scent of my beloved heaves me Godward. It's the Incarnation. God has taken on human form. God, born of a woman. Substance. Matter. Earth for God's body.

My grandfather used to call me "Stuff," and my uncle John called me "Stuff Stuff." A precious nickname, the origins of which I know nothing, but it means *substance*. My connection to the earth tells me I am earthbound, and that is where I find God. Physical and spiritual are of a piece.

The effect of a smell can conjure a feeling, a memory, or the intuitive sense of things, an uncanny awareness of sadness about nothing you can think of, or the weightiness of a place, or the unbearable homesickness for a moment lost. Before my husband and I married I kept him near by wearing his shirt, one that he had worn and that smelled of him.

What does God smell like? What does divine love smell like?

Our bodily existence, our earthy substance, exudes God, and is drafting with the scent of the Divine. Every day in all moments, all places, in this moment, we can smell God. Our life emanates divine presence. We call the Sacred One by many names, or miss God altogether, but God is right there in all earthy moments. All matter, and all material substance, bring us God. It's all about God. All God.

We don't always name God—some never do. But God is there in all of it. Everything. Our whole existence. Our purpose in life, my purpose, is to find God in the body, in this bit of earth that my mother named for herself. Her middle name is my first. Our name is Ruth.

Initiative for Prayer

Prayer as Olfactory Field Trip

Go to a variety of places with your journal in tow. Here are suggestions for journaling practices:

- Explore the scents of the spices in your kitchen.
- Dig in your yard with a trowel.
- Take a long walk in the woods.
- Visit a spa or health food organic store that sells essential oils or incense sticks. You might want to buy a few to take home and burn.
- Browse around in a candle shop or garden shop.

Smell everything, everywhere. Breathe deep. Remind yourself that you are breathing in the Divine.

Journal Practice

Write some notes about what you experience. Write the names of the items or scents, and particularly your reaction to them. Did any of them conjure memories? Did you feel any emotions? Desire? Were you stirred with any negativity, such as anger or irritation, at the smell of any of them? Did you think of people or places when you smelled them? Offer thanksgiving for the physical experience of God and God's visitation through scent.

"Mary took a pound of costly perfume made of pure nard, anointed Jesus' feet, and wiped them with her hair. The house was filled with the fragrance of the perfume" (John 12:3).

I can smell the earth in a petunia. A particular earth. The dark, musky soil of my grandfather's garden. A small plot on a city lot where houses were separated by but an alley-way. Arms spread wide and you could touch two houses. Tall narrow houses each with a postage-stamp yard. In his case, a garden.

With my nose in a petunia, I am transported. I can see both sets of knees, mine and his, bent into the ground, hands busy with trowels, digging, weeding, and shoveling dark earth. A small space gone glorious with hollyhocks and hydrangeas, off the back porch.

With my nose in a petunia, I make my visitation. With a jar of spice, a whiff of cloves, I greet him coming in the door. He would stop off at the pub on his way from the mill as his steelworker friends were prone to do. There he would be, his metal pail in hand, smelling of the cloves he had chewed on his way, to disguise the smell of beer on his breath.

The essence of Karl Evans. He arrives on a scent. A bit of clove and he's scooping me up, his short-bodied, ruddy-complexioned, gruff-voiced self. An unsuspecting waft from a petunia in the clay pot on my front steps, like a carpet ride, delivers me to his garden. I can remember him without effort, and he died before I was four. I don't have to cling to his memory, because earth and spice are my treasure trove of presence. In earth and spice, he clings to me. He shows up.

Essence. Extruded oils. Olfactory. Moments captured in a fragrance. Memory and meaning, all in a scent. Emotion-tinged smells. Homesick, when honeysuckle floats in on night air like a Pennsylvania summer. Wistful, with the mingling of tobacco and old books. An odd sensation. A curious provocation. Unforeseen knowing. Memory and meaning, all in a scent.

Mary had a pound of pure nard, "and the house was filled with the fragrance." Intense, warm, dark notes; the little house in Bethany smelled of India. Pure nard. A root, dug from the earth in the foothills of the Himalayas. A fibrous spindle exuding exquisite oil, exotic cargo in caravans brought by way of Persia. Nard. And Mary had some. A pound of pure nard. She opened it and poured it out on Jesus's feet at a dinner party in her own home. And all the house was stirred by the dense aroma of earth. All the guests alert and focused.

For some it conjured the dead. For some it was the fire of love. For others it aroused to anger. All of them, moved with heightened awareness from the essential oil of nard.

Judas was awhirl with weights and measures: one pound pure nard, three hundred denarii. Coins jingling in his purse, numbers banging in his head. Calculations. Reappropriations. Aghast at the extravagance. Angry at the year's worth of income, gone in a day. Judas smelled money.

Some smelled the dead. The nard mingled the moment with all the deaths, all the journeys to the grave, all the last anointings of lifeless limbs. The essence of extreme unction. Perhaps Martha was transported to her brother's deathbed. Perhaps the nard startled her with the stench of death, and the want to wail, as a mourner at a grave. A sudden inexplicable grief. Inexplicable, because there he sat, wining and dining, with Jesus. Her brother alive again, Lazarus, whom she bound for burial, and then unbound, when Jesus roared his name graveside, and he came out, grave clothes trailing behind him. For Martha and Lazarus, nard delivered an uncanny awareness that they are intimate with death, and the grave, and so, too, with the company of heaven.

Mary, with her pound of pure nard, is overcome with passion, and she worships. She pours it all out, thick and glistening, all of it, pure and weighty. She fills the whole house with the fragrance of love, exotic, and expensive, and exquisite.

This gospel writer tantalizes us with a highly provocative household vignette. He presses on us, stimulates with language of touch, and taste, and smell, so that we will sense the bodily presence of Jesus. The Gospel according to John begins with the Incarnation. John begins with: "The Word became flesh" (John 1:14). Now it is six days before the Passover, six days before the Crucifixion, and John coaxes us back to incarnation with a pound of pure nard. Jesus is the presence of God, the essence of God in the world. God in flesh. Before Crucifixion and Good Friday, before the events of Resurrection and Easter morning, there is the essential: Incarnation. God meeting us, in life, and in death. God with hands, and feet, and skin, and hair, and breath, and a scent.

Initiative for Prayer

Prayer as Sculpting

Acquire some modeling clay and gather some small tools from the kitchen or purchase some at an art store. The clay can be anything of your choice, and it can be air-drying, non-drying, or kiln- or oven-drying. Take your time; carve or shape the Christ. Remember, artistic expression is your own. It can be abstract, it can be just the face, or full body, or profile. It could be just the feet that Mary anointed with nard. The point is to come in contact with the like substance, touchable, body of Christ. God incarnate with form, like us.

Patrick of Ireland is attributed with the fourth-century poem that lauds the presence of God in earth and all created matter. He lists one thing after another in true Celtic form to celebrate God's presence and immediate accessibility, so immediate in fact that we are bound with Christ, in the body. We bind God to ourselves, the poem says, when we bind ourselves with "the stable earth, the deep salt sea, around the old eternal rocks" and God is present to us "in mouth of friend and stranger."[7]

My daughter Sally took every opportunity, when we were in Europe and she was seven years old, to light candles and, for some reason, to lie prostrate. Right there in the middle of everything—foreign language, pilgrim feet all around, on marble floor and ancient plank—she laid herself down. Lit a candle and hit the floor. Again and again. What did she like about that? Where did she get that idea? She didn't see me doing it, I don't do that. Or at least, I didn't until I saw her and felt inspired. Body prayer. Gesture. Flame. Heat. Melting wax. Ancient of Days. And no need to craft the particular syllables and consonants, because she said it all with her body. Of my three children, she has always been the least ready to give words. But there, in Italy and France, in cathedral and crypt, she was utterly at home, sprawled out on the floor.

We tell stories with our bodies. We pray with our bodies. We find God with our bodies. The theology of creation and incarnation affirms that this life in the body is a journey of sacred moments of discovering God in the material substance of the created world.

By virtue of the Incarnation, God is in and through and all around. God is in the room, and in the people around us; God is in the ground underfoot, in the smell of earthen floor. Incarnation gives us God to taste in wheat from the field and the fruit of the vine. Six days and counting, and Jesus is all about the nard, pouring it out and filling the house with its fragrance. All about keeping the feast. He is God with us in life, and in death, even when God is delivered in the stench of Lazarus four days in the grave, and calling for his unwrapping.

By virtue of the Incarnation, God has a smell. What does God smell like for you? Where do you find yourself surprised or curiously provoked? Or moved with an unforeseen knowing, stirred by a vague but heightened awareness of all the round earth, and the Divine Company in it? Sometimes when we smell God, we know it. Sometimes, when we smell God, we wince with a sense of sorrow or loss but don't know why. We may be aroused with anger, or overwhelmed with passion, but don't name God as the provocateur and miss the opportunity to engage directly with the Holy Incarnate One.

What does Divine Love smell like? God has come into the world. Will we find God in it, and know it? Incarnation invites us to begin recognizing God in a scent that drifts our way. God in a body opens the opportunity to love like Mary, or to be combative like Judas, but whatever scent presents itself, make God your go-to, to rejoice, to pour out love, to debate, to do battle, or rile against, but in all of it, in any of it, God is present in that trace aroma. Will we extract the essential oil, the precious essence of God, from all that is around us? Will we dig for roots in the foothills of the Himalayas?

Judas weighed, and measured, and counted the cost, and reappropriated. Mary poured it all out for the love of God. Here. Now. In and for this moment.

Initiative for Prayer

Prayer as Sensual Soul-Searching and Intellectual Consideration

After a quick errand to the backyard, garden spot, or nursery center, place a mound of earth in front of you and think about these words: humility, humble, humus, human.

Using your senses as stimulus for prayerful contemplation, consider the Baptismal Covenant and this promise that we make: "Will you strive for justice and peace among all people, and respect the dignity of every human being?" [8]

Take the question apart and prayerfully examine the meaning of the words. Write these phrases down the margin of one page in your prayer journal, with some space in between. Write your thoughts in the space beside each.

- Strive for
- Justice
- Peace
- Will you?
- All People
- Respect
- Dignity
- Every
- Human Being

Write a summary paragraph about how this might influence your life as you walk about in this world, and how it might prepare you to find the Incarnate Christ.

My day got ahead of me, so I didn't get out for a run until the sun was high in the sky, and the temperature registered eighty-two degrees. A bit warm for a run, but just right for the heavy scents of spring, weighty and voluptuous, privet hedge and honeysuckle both floating on the breeze. I don't know the chemistry of air, or how heat changes the air into a structure that can do this heavy lifting, or if in fact that's how it works at all, but I'm a romantic, so it makes me think of the offertory sentence, "Walk in love as Christ loved us and gave himself for us, a fragrant offering and sacrifice, to God."[9]

What a mystery. The changed structure of resurrection-laden air. We've been to the grave, and beyond our knowing, Christ has been raised; his heavy scent, weighty and voluptuous, rises with the heat of the paschal fire, and it gets all over us. Resurrected love. Somehow, it has a scent. And we smell of it.

People who haven't been around the fire, know that we have, because they can smell it on us. They can get it too, the love of Christ. All the world can know the love of Christ, because we walk with resurrected love, and they can smell it on us. The household is heady with the fragrance of divine love, simply because we walked through the room, and they can smell the love. The neighborhood is sensitive to the presence of the divine, because the love of Christ exudes from our pores, and drifts on a breeze, invisible, but making certain of an unmistakable sacred presence. The world is tilting a curious head, for an uncanny, recognizable, but yet unidentified Holy Fragrance because we are walking in love.

We carry our incense-pierced pillar candle in procession, because we know what that paschal fragrance is, and we delight in it. It is the victory of love. It is life over death. It is mortality putting on immortality. It is divine love. It is the light of Christ. It is our routine Sunday love affair.

2

THE SPIRITUALITY
OF STACKING STONES

Camping in the Sierras at ten thousand feet. Bedrock, save for the mules that packed in for us, carrying our tent, sleeping bags, and thin inflatable mattress pads. Besides that, our camp stove, two camp chairs, a small table that rolls up, a cooler of perishables, and a duffle bag of freeze-dried dinners in foil packets. The perishables allowed for unparalleled breakfasts of sausage patties and pancakes, or biscuits if we preferred, with eggs and piping hot coffee in a percolating pot, poured into tin cups, with milk. Extraordinary luxuries.

We decided over breakfast what to do with our day. Italy Pass. That would be our first day, a hiking day. Yesterday had been all mule saddle, setting up campsite, rigging the bear pulley, and a bit of fishing around the rim of Honeymoon Lake. Today we would hike.

The map said that Italy Pass was not a well-marked hiking trail. We saw at least one or two carved wooden signs in the shape of a point for an arrow, so we knew the general direction. We had a map and compass; we would give it our best shot. Worst-case scenario we would enjoy the spectacular scenery and wind our way back to camp, the way we came.

Jacob dreamed of a ladder at heaven's gate when he slept with his head on a rock for a pillow. And despite our notions of the charming stable of wood timbers, Jesus was, most likely, born in a cave, a hollow in rock. Or at least he was cradled in one, the manger a trough for feeding livestock, chiseled stone. Rock to manifest the presence of God.

Rock. The stuff of God revealed. Heaven to earth come down. The eastern slope of the glorious Sierra Mountains. Magnificently barren. Ancient, and rugged, and stunningly beautiful. Rock under every step, the view in every direction. Just rock to sit, or lean, or pull yourself up on, or lie down on at night. My husband, Benno, said, "If Jesus had been born and raised in the Sierras, he would've picked up a rock, instead of bread, and said, 'This is my body.'" The world would have understood perfectly that God is in that rock. His Celtic sensibility that God is present in the body in earth, and rock, and all matter of things, whether the fruit of the earth in bread and wine, or in the substance of the earth itself, in rock and stone.

Rock. Ancient and eternal, the beginning and the end. Fortress and crag; stronghold; refuge and hiding place. Safety, security, sustaining. Immovable, unshakeable, abundantly beneath, before, behind, above, below. Silent and strong. Tumbling in avalanche and quarry-like. Arranged in caverns, and craters for cupping lakes. Stacked like steps as though they're expecting your pilgrim feet. Rocks big enough to not despair the lack of shade trees. Resting in the shadow to eat our lunch, and lean.

Stones, small enough to pick up and stack in delightful little cairns, which is what the "not well marked" designation meant for the trail to Italy Pass. Nothing but little stacks of stones, three, four, five inches high; rocks not easily seen against a backdrop of rock. It was more like hunting Easter eggs than seeing signposts. We hiked, climbed, and rested our way up to nearly twelve thousand feet by way of a four-mile, not-well-marked trail. It was not a trail, really, at all. It simply was, a way. A way through the rocks to more rocks. Steeper rocks. Mountains of rock, and slopes between mountains, called passes. Deposits of rock that take shape like the clouds, and bear the names of images, like Julius Caesar, Miriam, Four Peaks, and Bear Spire. A way through the rocks with rocks to mark the way.

For some strange reason I began to feel that the hikers and pilgrims who stacked the cairns were women, or at least, in some way, feminine. I felt the presence of those who went before, as though they played with us by stacking stones. Nymphs inviting. Muses inspiring. Mischievous elves knocking the stacks down to make the trail go still. Companions, keeping us safe. Beckoning. Gesturing. Including. Such delight. Our silent company. Watching for their signs, following them foreword, telling us to turn sharp or turn back a way, or to go down again, and then go up. Our Divine Company. God with a backdrop of God.

Though I am a novice hiker, eventually I felt frisky enough that I could join the throng of adventurers who forged this trail with their cairns, and I added here and there a little stone of my own, like playing the secretary game when someone whispers a secret and says, "Pass it on." That's what we did.

We added little stones of our own. Our marked steps. Our day trip. Our journey by foot in the Sierras. No matter that we are novice pilgrims. Our journey is worth making. Our story is worth telling. The stones help us tell it. All pilgrims are alike in one thing, we are all making a way through the rocks, with rocks to mark the way.

The stones along the way bear witness to our presence there, at Honeymoon Lake, sleeping on rocks beneath the stars, or luxuriating over breakfast in feather jackets before the sun climbed its way over stone peaks, or resting at a glacier lake that suddenly appeared like the earth's chalice offering up strong drink of God, when we've reached a high enough elevation to see over its rim.

Initiative for Prayer

Prayer as Remembering and Storytelling

Storytelling in stone. Gather a basket of stones and rocks, any sizes, colors, or textures. First, contemplate the rocks. Pick them up, smell them, feel them, press them to your cheek, lay them out on a surface, and move them around in random arrangements. You might want to do this, now and then, for a few days before moving on. Jacob turned a stone on end to stand as a memorial, to remember where it was that he slept at heaven's gate, right there in the rock beneath his head.

Now begin by choosing one, and then another, up to as many as you like, and let them bring to mind life moments for you. Think like Jacob and arrange them as ancient holy companions to your life that tell your story. If you like working with a friend or partner, tell each other the stories the stones told you.

When your children ask their parents in time to come, "What do these stones mean?" then you shall let your children know, "Israel crossed over the Jordan here on dry ground." (Joshua 4:21–22)

Stones that hold meaning. Rocks that hold memory. Joshua set up twelve stones, heavy souvenirs, from the dry ground at the bottom of a river. A ritual of rock to remember when they walked through water and never got wet. A memento in Gilgal, so their children would think to ask, "What do these stones mean?" With their memories jogged, they would tell the story of how they knew God. Jacob stacked stones on the ground where he wrestled an angel to the dislocation of his own hip. A spirituality of stacking stones, to mark, to memorialize, to remember why he changed his name.

Rocks and stones; the people of God, and their stories.

Five smooth stones. The boy David, who would be king, collected them from the stream to carry in his pouch for slinging. One of them he flung across a battlefield and embedded in the forehead of a giant. I can imagine him carrying the unused four in his pocket, with which to tell the story to his friends.

Moses striking water from a rock, and tablets of stone, scripted stones, chiseled letters, words from God in stone thrown down, and broken. Moses, tucked away in the cleft of a rock to be protected from seeing too much of the Holy One straight on, so God's glory wouldn't inadvertently smite him. Stones with meaning, rocks that hold memory.

The people of God singing, and praying in psalms, about rocks: the crag of a rock, a cliff, a cleft, a hiding crevice in the desert. Poems remembering when God showed God's own self, and when God spoke, telling about when God acted mighty to save the people, or when they were sheltered instead—in the rock.

A rolling stone that closed a tomb. A heavy stone that caused women to wonder who would move it, so they could spice their beloved's body. His lifeless body laid on a human-sized stone slab at burial, and an angel that sat relaxed on top of the other stone successfully rolled away, so the women could explore the fresh earth of resurrection. Hollow stone, and tunnels in rock, to hide the faithful and newly baptized. Stories painted, and graphed, in catacombs of rock, under Rome.

Autobiography in a series of stones. Spiritual stories. A ritual of rock that holds meaning.

I never know what to do with the rocks my children collect. This inherent need to pick up a chunk of the earth's crust to validate their existence and authenticate their adventures. Rocks from the park, and playground, a baggie of rubble from their trip to London. Palm-sized stones from Rome tucked in our luggage in a little zippered pouch from Paris. We are weighted down with memory. How could I discard them? The small hands that collected them, the bulging pockets that toted them, my children's hearts, foolish enough to think they're treasures. Rocks that hold my story, and help me tell it: "This is where I went; let me tell you what happened there." Time distances us from events and erases the details. But piles of rocks, and the practice of telling our stories, help us to remember.

Ancient Celtic peoples carved stories in stone and raised them as monuments, the high crosses, to stand "as a focal point in the countryside, claiming the land for Christ, making a statement of belief in the possibility of a transfigured universe."[10] Newell writes about the symbolism of the familiar shape of the Celtic cross, how it "holds together its love of Christ and its love of creation by combining the images of the cross and the orb, invites us to see Christ and creation coming forth from the same point, both emerging from the Heart of God. Christ comes to reconnect us to that Heart, to the Unity from which all life comes."[11]

A grieving family created a memorial garden in a public museum house. Among the flowers that recalled their mother's love for life and her life-long love affair with flowers, they placed a well-chosen rock, practically boulder-sized, and bolted to it a plaque with her name. In memory of. A visiting place. A place to meander, and sift through memories, and laugh, and relive, or to pick up the sorrow and grieve awhile.

The burden of grief is exhausting. We carry it like a boulder, too precious to put down, too heavy to hold. A rock that holds the memory of the dead gives me rest from my grief. We can leave it at that rock knowing the memory will be preserved. The stone that tells our story for us helps us to remember, and at the same time allows us the safety to relax into forgetfulness, because we know the rock will remember for us. It will keep our place. Our story is preserved. Our lives are marked with a series of stones.

Stacked stones formed crude altars for the ancients, slabs of stone formed altar tables for the early church, big enough for a body to lie down. Big enough for a community to gather round to share a meal, and tell their stories, and remember their saving events. Stones that hold meaning, rocks that hold memory. If we don't mark the places in our lives when God wrestled us, or took us dry through deep waters, if we don't tell our stories with a series of stones, will we ever know that God was there, with us, along the way? Without the rocks that help us remember our lives, would we cultivate hearts that are foolish enough to consider them treasures? Would we remember how God's arm moved on our behalf to save us, or when God hid us to keep us safe? Would we ever remember how many times we've been saved? Without the stones, who would know to prod us by asking: "What do these stones mean?" (Joshua 4:21), just so we can tell our story out loud, and remember. Without the stones, we wouldn't tell our stories about God, and we wouldn't remember, anymore.

We come from a long line of people who set out stones that have meaning, rocks that hold memory. Lay your story in stone. Lay it down in rocks that remember. Write it with a series of stones, a veritable stack of stones, that mark the moments, when . . .

————

Initiative for Prayer

Prayer as Daily Pilgrimage
and Marking Places to Remember

Collect five to fifteen small stones or three larger stones. Think strategically about your daily routine. Stack some stones, somewhere, in a place in or around your residence, as a secret marker to yourself. Small stones to measure four or five inches high, or big stones pulled out of the earth. You might want to set out more than one stack, perhaps two or three or four stacks.

As you see the stack of stones when you pass them by in your daily routine, what do they say to you? How do they greet you? What do they remind you of or make you think about? Ask the stones to tell you where God is in this day, or to help you remember your story. How are the stones different from day to day? How do they tell the story of your week? In what way do they help you find your way? What do they tell? Jot down a few thoughts.

————

3

GUARDIAN IN CLAY

The childhood years, elementary school. Taking papers home and bringing them back. Signed permission slips. A doctor's excuse or tardy note. The census. And of course, report cards. All of them needing signatures.

In those days we didn't have to verify our residence in triplicate in order to be admitted; everyone went to the neighborhood school, except for some of the Catholic kids who went to St. Elizabeth's. And they had to pay money. No one doubts who you are if you pay money. But there were papers, forms from school to be signed by a parent. And there it was, looming large on the page. That one word. There. Under that line, where it says "Sign Here: Parent or Guardian."

Guardian. Like a silent threat. Scalding. Menacing, and dangerously close to a real possibility, that I could end up with a guardian. That's for children with no parents at all, and I was down one. One to go. Made me want to cover my paper like it was something scandalous or obscene. Shameful. Who of my schoolmates would think a parent could die? Did the other children know my mother was dead? Was it still a secret? Did they even know what the word "guardian" meant, and did my paper flash neon like a warning beacon, for everyone to flee?

A guardian angel wasn't something our household believed in, but it sounded enticing to have an angel whose sole charge was me, following me around, making up disguises to fit in, fighting the bullies, whispering orders, befriending wild animals, and giving me a lift when the wind speed was just right. There probably was no such-a-thing. Guardian angels. Besides, I was afraid of angels and prayed I would never see one. Also, I asked God, please, to never show up in a form that I could see. That would have scared the daylights out of me.

One parent shy of the need for a guardian, a housekeeper was the next best thing. A stand-in. A temp. "I'm your mother now," until I leave and the ad goes back in the paper for another housekeeper. Caregiver for four children. Care and maintenance. Meals. Laundry. House cleaning. Packing lunches. Custodial care and maintenance. Less care and more maintenance. Sometimes, just maintenance.

Housekeepers. Thirteen in seven years. Then none. From the time I was three until I was ten. My life a wilderness. An uninhabitable place. A place where no one wants to live. They always left in short order.

I wanted someone to do battle for me. Guard. Defend. Champion in the world. One who sends you out in the morning, sends you on your way with a blessing. At least a vote of confidence. "I know you can do it." "Knock 'em dead." "Hit it out of the park." That's what mothers do.

Mothers don't always do that, but I wanted mine to do it for me. Guard. Defend. Champion. I imagined that's what mothers did. Good mothers. And surely, all mothers are good. At least mine would be. If she had been here.

I like to think myself a good mother. I don't always guard, defend, champion, but I want to. I want to give that to my children: "I know what you are made of, and it is good."

If the classroom occasion forced an explanation from me, I always said, "I don't have a mother," as if there was a living breathing being walking the face of the earth that didn't have a mother. But it sounded better than saying, "My mother is dead." What a notion, that a mother was something I didn't have. Like I didn't have any lunch money, or a pencil. Coming up short. Insufficient funds. Doing without. Making do. Inadequate to the task. Finding alternatives.

It's all language of deficiency. All of it reflecting on me. Depleted. Which is defined by Merriam-Webster as "emptied of a principal substance."[12] For me, the principal substance was flesh and blood, body and bone, matter. Matter. Mother. Of the same substance. I wanted one who was of my same stuff. My matter. My mother. My flesh and blood, my body and bone. I wanted someone to do battle for me. Guard. Defend. Champion in the world. Bless and cheer me. Of the same substance.

To say that Jesus was born of a woman means that he is of the same substance, same stuff as his mother, and is of the same human substance as me. Both of us born of a mother. My humanity, my existence, of one kind with the bread of heaven. God, born of a woman, flesh and blood, body and bone. Same stuff. Earth, and clay, and humus. God incarnate. Same stuff. My stuff.

Initiative for Prayer

Meditation and Theological Reflection as Prayer

Reflect on the Incarnation by meditating on this phrasing from the Nicene Creed:

"For us and for our salvation he came down from heaven:

by the power of the Holy Spirit he became incarnate from the Virgin Mary,

and was made man."[13]

Feed your prayerful imagination. Look up a variety of artists' depictions of Mary the mother of Jesus. Seek a broad representation and media, such as modern art, abstract art, the classics, early church, the Renaissance, multicultural, Russian or Greek Orthodox icons, paintings, sculptures, mosaics. Compare and contrast the images. What strikes you; what surprises you or pleases you? What do you dislike? What do we know about Mary simply because of how artists have depicted her? What had you not thought of before, about Mary or about the Incarnation? How do your thoughts change about Mary or about Jesus, or about yourself? In your journal, write some of your thoughts. Try some drawing of your own. What does that feel like? What does it mean to you that Jesus is substance and matter, flesh and bone, like you?

Jesus was led up by the Spirit into the wilderness to be tempted by the devil. He fasted for forty days and forty nights, and afterwards he was famished. (Matthew 4:1–2)

The earth dances in delight. Daffodils, forsythia, and dandelions, a triptych of glory trundling at the curb anxious to make their Alleluia announcement. Yard weeds strewn like lavender fields. God in gutter garb, eager to be seen. All the round earth reveals the Divinity. The Holy One, in form and substance. The Incarnate One, fashioned of mud and clay. God as earthenware.

The earth dances in delight because the earth already knows, and so do we. The season of Epiphany revealed it to us, the mystery of the word made flesh. "In the mystery of the Word made flesh, you have caused a new light to shine in our hearts, to give the knowledge of your glory in the face of your Son Jesus Christ our Lord."[14]

From the beginning of Epiphany to the end, from his Holy Baptism to his Transfiguration, God is revealed. Nine weeks of light, and glory, and seeing, and knowing. And with the slight smudge of mortality, a thumb-print of ash on our foreheads, we suspend our alleluias, and hush the glory of heaven to earth come down. All the round earth is silenced, and what we know about God turns to what we don't know about being human. Lent is all about the earth part.

My Thursday morning book group gave me a gift that carries an incredible insight into the Incarnation. They bought it from an artisan who crafts guardian angels and names them for their bearers. The one they chose for me is called "the guardian angel of those who follow creeks and streams." The head and body are fashioned of clay. Mud baked in fire, then glazed, then outfitted with seed pods for wings, and a glorious broad spread fungus for a halo behind the head. The clay arms reach out and form a heavy-laden basket brimming with moss, and rocks, and bits of creek bed, and a rusty fragment for a sword, propped against the shoulder.

Angels are warriors you know. Why else would we have come to call them guardians? There stands my angel on the windowsill with a message for me about incarnation: the guardian rises up out of the very stuff he comes to guard.

And so it is, with the Incarnate God, mucking about in human form. Rising up out of earth, and ash, and posturing in clay. This incarnate, earthenware God, takes us into the heart of our humanity, because we don't understand about being human. Holy mud. Sacred matter. Baked clay. It's all about earth. And Lent is our season to get inside of it. Jesus, with his forty days and nights in the wilderness, and the wilderness where Jesus lived, is nothing but raw earth.

I've been there. Three times, as a matter of fact, to the very same wilderness of the Jesus saga. The landscape is stunning and unforgettable. The wilderness for Jesus was the Judean desert. In topographical terms, the wilderness is a descent into the earth. In a distance of just fifteen miles from Jerusalem to the Dead Sea, the annual rainfall drops from twenty-five inches to two. The landscape descends 3,700 feet. The climate warms you in winter, scorches you in summer, and chills you at night. Your own body is an oasis to the air around you, leaving your skin parched and salty, and your mouth dry as sand. It is a place of whirlwinds, thorns, and pits, a haunt for jackals and vultures. Beasts live there. It is otherwise uninhabitable.

Our poets and prophets use wilderness, as metaphor of course, to mean a lonely place. Or to say that something is laid waste, or that it is ruined, or deserted, or destroyed. Or to talk about a place where no one wants to live, and yet, some prophets have seen God there. And some have known God to speak; the word of the Lord came to John the Baptist in the wilderness, and to Elijah at the edge of a cave.

The terrain is dramatic and dangerous. Extraordinarily rugged jutting cliffs on bare heights; winding paths, and gullies for getting lost, or for hiding. Deep weaving caverns, tight crevices, and crags, so that, in the wilderness, you are, in effect inside the earth. You are at 1,200 feet below sea level. Jesus makes his way into the depths of the earth, into the depths of our humanity, and he does battle for us there, in the wilderness.

If we sort of psychoanalyze the dialogue between Jesus and the devil, it's a classic, and we could say that the wilderness event is about identity. Two functioning parts of identity for all of us are the questions: Who am I? and Who is God? The temptations are simple scenarios at the most basic level of identity and existence. They get at our concerns about sustenance, and safety, and the ability to act, and whether or not we have any significance in the world. And they complicate things with matters of cruelty, control, and the plight of powerlessness, as we scrap to figure out the delicate balances of human life and identity.

Theological banter regarding Jesus's temptations in the wilderness can lead us to a conversation about sin and bend us around to the path of Augustine's emphasis on sin, and fallen humanity, and total depravity. Celtic theology opens a conversation about the goodness of humanity: discovering that we are made from God, and like this Incarnate Holy One, the divine light within us cannot be overcome. We are of God and blessed by God, so that Jesus meeting us in the wilderness means he is one of us, can enter into the struggle with us, and companion us to find the beauty of our earthen clay form.

Celtic spirituality inspires me with the concept "that what is deepest in us is the image of God. God's wisdom is born with us 'in the womb,' as Ecclesiasticus says, or as John says, in us is 'the true light that enlightens everyone coming into the world.' Sin has buried the beauty of God's image, but not erased it."[15]

Jesus heals with mud and spittle, touch and words, and it hints at our shared humanity, and that we are made of the same stuff as he. It hints at his identity as the Word, through which all things came to be. It hints at the truth that healing and resurrection are the overcoming acts of all forms of death, and are variable forms of God's creative acts. Celtic spirituality would hold that creation and incarnation are God's saving acts, in as much as is his death on the cross and his resurrection from the grave.

All of creation, all of humanity, all things which have been made, were not made without the presence, and participation, of the Incarnate One, and the Holy Spirit, whom we call Wisdom. I think we could see it if we can imagine Jesus standing with us, as he did with the blind man, the both of us covered in mud. When we don't know who we are, and who God is, it can lay waste to our lives. When we don't understand that we are the beloved of God, and that God is the source of life and resides in all physical life, including our own, we can settle for a hard life of desert wilderness, and reside in lonely uninhabited places of desolation and ruin.

Lent is all about the element of earth, and we are earthenware. We hold back our alleluias, because alleluias hail the Resurrection. Lent hails the Incarnation, and the humanity of Jesus. Jesus is born of a woman and like her, in her humanity, he is subject to death. Jesus is making his way into the depths of the earth, even to the depths of the grave, to find us. He is coming into the wilderness, into the heart of our humanity, to keep us. To guard, defend, champion. And to teach us what we need to know about being human, which is the Eden-Gethsemane garden truth that we are born of God, in the image of God, and that we retain the inherent goodness declared by God when God created us. Jesus has taken on the form and substance of that which he came to save. Lent is his searching of cavern, and crevice, and all the wilderness to bring us out. He will do battle for us there. Our guardian in clay. He will do battle to save the goodness of humanity.

O God of Black Earth with dirt in hand, who fashions humanity from dust and ash, grant that we may delight in the smooth, dark faces, sandstone brows, and crystalline cheekbones of your humanity, that we might know you, as we see them. Amen.

Initiative for Prayer

Prayer as Play

Make a party of it and make mud pies. Make clay figures and bake them in the sun. Enter a muddy buddy race. Revel in your earthenware self. Welcome yourself as the beloved of God, as one who is worth coming for, worth doing battle for, and worth finding. You are worth fighting for in the battle with death.

Body Prayer

Touch the sign of the cross on your own body. If you have children, teach your children how to cross themselves, as a sign that you are "holy and acceptable to God,"[16] and that you are of God, and belong to God. In case you don't know how to do it, it goes like this:

Touch your fingertips to your forehead.

Then to your belly.

Across to your left shoulder, then to your right shoulder.

Finish by touching to the center at your breastbone.

This can also be a prayer for any of us when we want the feeling of having that guardian in clay, like a secret holy sign language to tell your guardian that you know he is close at hand.

4

DORSEY AND JIM

I am flying into the sun, and I keep hoping it means I am getting younger. It's earlier than it was before. I met my beloved in midlife so I know a thing or two about time. I visited a newborn last week when he was but twenty-four hours old, and already, now he is nine days. But, oh, to have the luxury of measuring the newness of a life in hours or days. At the risk of sounding simplistic, as I left the hospital room I offered my sappy, sage advice: "Stay in the moment."

I wanted to guard them from the thing that robs me. Worry, anxiety, and concern about the morrow. Staying in the present is a challenge for me. I am a worrier. The anxiety of any given day has the potential to snatch away delight, beauty, and the richness that is actually in every day, somewhere, in some moment or piece of it.

I don't know if you've encountered it with children, but it seems that schools and organizations give away today in preparation for an ever-advancing tomorrow, as if borrowing from the future by robbing the present will make the children readier when it comes. I want to lobby for all children everywhere to have today their own right now. I guess in part because I want my own right now "right now." I don't want to lose today. I've lost a bunch of them already. I want to live into today like there is no tomorrow. And when tomorrow comes it will be the wonderful new today.

I know this all sounds simplistic, but it is my growing edge. My daily practice, to let go of angst about tomorrow or all the "what ifs" about my children, and stay present to today with a big fat glorious embrace. Monks had it figured out. The way to live a day, to embrace it, to cling to it, to be present to it, and to stay in it was to pray it. They called it marking the hours of the day, and they divided a day into about eight or nine segments and named them. You've probably heard some of the names like matins or vespers. To live a holy life was to live a holy day, and to live a holy day was to pray the hours of it. An hour is holy for no other reason than because the Holy One is in it.

We're not monks, and we don't live in monasteries, but we still want to treasure a day, and slow it down, and be present to it. So, the church has whittled it down for us, to three hours of the day plus one for goodnight: Morning Prayer, Noonday Prayer, Evening Prayer, and Compline. We want to stay present. We want to savor and salvage all the moments, because eventually we have to stop measuring their lives in hours or days or weeks or months because we start lighting candles for one year, and then a bunch of years. God is present in this moment, to be counted as the one moment that matters. Right now.

Celtic sensibilities fundamentally heighten our awareness of the presence of God in the moment, and in the immediacy of the life we are living. Kate and Grace lead us, my sister Barbara and me, on a day-retreat to a stone circle in County Donegal, during my self-directed Celtic pilgrimage. Grace said that if she had to get at the essence or meaning of Celtic spirituality in a word, it would be the word "presence." The presence of God in the very breath you breathe, the sky above your head, the earth under your feet, and this road you're standin'on, right here. It is full of God. You can find God here. Now. Here, anywhere.

Celtic spirituality is the practice of attentiveness and staying present. God is in this moment, so you be in it, too. You, be present, and you will see God, find God, know God, right here and now. No moment or place is bereft of God, and Celtic prayers claim it, and Celtic practices live into that certainty, boldly, with celebration and simplicity.

Esther de Waal considers this to be "perhaps the most important" gift from the Celtic tradition,

> this vivid sense of a God who knows, loves, supports, is close at hand, and actually present in their lives. . . . They speak of God dwelling in his world, and in our lives in such a way that Emmanuel, God with us, becomes a reality. . . . This is a God physically present, alongside, behind, before, above, below. God is companion, guest, fellow traveler, friend, fellow worker. Some of the most-used words that

we find in these prayers are *encircle, encompass, uphold, surround*. This flows from their real, lived-out grasp of the centrality of the incarnation.[17]

Praying the hours can be the big fat hugging of today—immersion in the present because that is where God is. I know a thing or two about time. I want to fly into the sun, because I want it to be earlier than it was. I want to have the fresh young wedding day with Benno, that Dorsey and Jim invited me to bless for them. I want all the yesterdays back to do them differently.

But we have today. Simple morning, noon, and night, and prayers to give us a whole life lived, in a day. Benno is my life. My joy, my play, my rapture; my rock, my climbing from a bitter cold stream when I need to regain the feeling in my feet. He is my hiding place and fortress, my praying, and my finding God's sacred presence in this incarnate life.

The old prayer book liturgies for marriage have been scrapped, wisely tossed; that stuff about obedience, and women being property. But somebody from back then had one thing figured out, that marriage is our way into the holy mysteries of Incarnation, and God's invitation to our knowing. So, one line I keep, because they let you say: "With my body I thee Worship." Our names, Benno + Ruth, chiseled in old eternal rock. For all time. And from before time. I will live my whole life today in one day, in this day, with Benno. That is my solemn vow. Notes, jotted down on a plane, from Georgia to Oregon.

Initiative for Prayer

Body Prayer: Hot Stones for Prayer with a Partner

Gather several smooth black stones, palm-sized. Garden centers sell these individually or by the bag. Place them in a stone or ceramic mixing bowl. Boil some water. Pour the water over the stones and let them soak for a few minutes. Use tongs to take them out of the hot water and wrap them in a towel. Let the rocks cool enough that they will not burn to the touch.

One partner lies face down on the floor, on a yoga mat or folded blanket. The other places another towel over the back of the other, then on the towel arranges the hot rocks over back, neck and shoulders, small of the back, and hips. As a body prayer, focus on the bodily experience of God in these rocks. Find God in this experience. Find God in the weight. Find God in the heat. Be, in God. If it helps, imagine God as some of these:

God as hiding place and refuge.

God as ancient of days and knowing.

God as rest and retreat.

God in the weight, and real substance of hot rocks.

Reflections for Dorsey and Jim on Their Wedding Day

The Lord is my rock, my fortress, and my deliverer, my God, my rock in whom I take refuge. (Psalm 18:2)

I've just returned from two weeks in my home place, and from romping with my three children in the mountains around our cottage in Ligonier, Pennsylvania. We spent a day at a woodland stream, a favorite spot for trout fishermen. All of us fishing with the hopes of reeling in a big one, but spending a more whole-hearted effort at finding ways of falling in. Summer heat had no measure. As refreshing as the water was, it was so cold I had to climb an enormous rock in the middle to regain the feeling in my feet. After several retreats to the rock, I noticed that someone else had been there before, and left their mark.

There, etched in the rock, a heart, and the letters K S L + M S Y with a frame around it, including decorative corner angles, an arrow through it, flower above it, and the date: 1926. Ah, love. The extraordinary mystery. But great length, and no little trouble to these young lovers in 1926, to carve their love, for time and eternity, in a rock. Love, all for love, these crevices quarried out of the rock one chip at a time.

They were pioneers in their own right, foraging their way through wilderness, with nothing but love and something to carve rock. Romantic bliss, blind love, impulsive, powerful flame, and fire of love, worthy of the poetry of the Song of Solomon.

The anonymous young love birds of 1926, now sage and seasoned, patinaed like the rock itself, and like all the sages gathered to wed the two of you, would tell you, you'll need plenty more than love. You'll need a sense of responsibility, and a good dose of duty, endurance, and patience. You'll need a roof over your heads and food on your table. You'll need the heart of a servant, and some self-sacrifice, a flare for drama, and company. You'll need mutuality, a grand sense of humor, and a broad capacity for beauty.

The disciple who wrote the gospel account and the letter we call First John was someone who has seen, heard, and touched Jesus, and he inscribed a new definition of love. John says, "God is love" (1 John 4:8). Simple as that, there it is. Three words: God is Love. John would have it that all you need for your life together is found, and resourced, in God. For this reason, you are here, today, in the church. You don't need a church to get married. You don't even need a priest, and surely not two, let alone strings, organ, and choir, all of which are exquisite. You are here in this way because you want to get what the church gives. And that is God's blessing on your marriage. We pronounce God's name over you with raised hand and symbolic gesture. Theologically, it means that God will move out and all around you to envelope and fill you. God will exercise God's power, and love, within you. God will move you to love, and God will be that love inside of you when your resources run thin. It means that God, through whom "all things came into being" (John 1:3), this God will call you, and your relationship, good. That's what the blessing of God means. It is his presence there, in your marriage, that will make it good. God in you, God between, before, behind you. God above and beside you. That's it. That's what you've come here for.

You will make your promises and exchange rings just like anyone can do with a justice of the peace, in a backyard or on a riverboat. But we, here in the church, will bless those rings. Then at the altar rail, we will bless you. And God will go with you, and before you, and God will live in you.

That's what this is all about. You are getting all you need to make it from here. Dorsey and Jim, I'd like you to take this image of God with you. It is the image of the love rock from my Pennsylvania stream. Let today be your etching. Dig in deep and secure your love in the rock. God is love. The psalmists are passionate, and they use lovers' language, and they call God their rock. Carve your names in the person of God in creation. God is a firm place to hold to, and to cling. He is steady, and unmoved by storms, snow, ice, and beating sun. God is your rock, strong and broad above the waters, but in them too. God is a place to retreat to and hear nothing but the rush of living water. God is a place to rest in your love, and find your leisure, where your reality is transformed, and meals are called picnics, and bathing is called skinny dipping. God is a place to climb, slick, and weathered just enough, to give you the thrill of a slip when you need to cool off in white water. God is your rock. A hiding place when you are afraid. A refuge when you are in danger. A fortress when you need to battle outside forces. God is all of these. God is your rock, your ancient of days rising up out of the earth's core and surfacing its crust in white waters.

Today is your day of going there to inscribe your names. To put your love there, to find your love there. All of it. In God.

Initiative for Prayer

Prayer as Place: Wordless Prayer

Find a big boulder. Perhaps on a playground or in a neighbor's rock garden, or someplace near a river bank, or find a stone wall. Again, it might be along your neighborhood walk, or in a church, library, museum, or cemetery. Use your body for meditation, and contemplation, which is to say, use your body to experience God as rock. Sit. Lean. Touch the stone with whole open hands. Curl up. Stand, lean, lie down, on the rock of your finding.

Experience the rock. Be inspired. Listen to the rock with your body. Feel the physical qualities of the Rock. What are they? The psalmists call God their rock. The image of God as rock bids the experience of God as place, rather than God as person. Explore that idea of God as place by positioning yourself, silent and motionless, on the rock. What do you find there? Scribble a few words in your journal, or just draw some rocks and boulders.

Barbara and I got tickled at ourselves going all round about in Ireland taking pictures of rocks and rubble. Tickled at the ridiculousness of it. Piles of rocks, lines of rocks, stones stacked up to make fences, enormous stones carved to make high crosses that tell stories, stone hollowed out to make a font, or stacked high to make round bell towers in keeping with Celtic tradition. Ah more rocks, let's look at these rocks over here, and take more pictures that will be indistinguishable one from another in a travel journal photo album. Rocks, we call ruins, and more ruins.

We heard ourselves size up the value of a place or structure by how old it was. A two-hundred-year-old stone cottage, lovely, and quaint, but not so very old. Ah, but here, a cathedral built in the thirteenth century. And this, a tiny stone church from the tenth century, just one wall and a doorway, still standing. But this, now, here's something ancient. A stone, dug up, from maybe a sixteen-hundred-year-old site where there was once a well . . . maybe, belonging to Patrick himself. And then there were ancient stone circles, and Stonehenge, mysteriously old, and mysteriously purposed, and possibly even enticingly pagan.

You become self-conscious about it all, and begin to wonder why it matters. To you. Or at all, to anyone. These crumbling Celtic church sites. Ruins. Things lie in ruin. Stones stacked and tumbling. Why our fascination? Do we need it because it is evidence that we lived a life? Proof that something important happened here? Something that once was, but isn't anymore? Joshua would have it that the stones hold memory, and tell the story. But what is that story?

When our retreat leader talked about the Celtic notion of listening to the earth, and what the earth might say about what it wants to become, or the stones, sinking back into the ground, and wondering what they want to do next, it occurred to me that for all the ancient sites and structures, and however old they are, that the very stones themselves are billions of years old. And that it's only for the last eight hundred years that one particular stone was part of a cathedral, or a manger or trough, or now, a pasture wall for keeping sheep. Stones, the rocks and ruins that are evidence of God present, not in history necessarily, but in the very earth. They are outcroppings of God rising from the green hills, evidence of our life in God, and God's cradling our existence. The hard-baked clay of bricks that take shape around us in a church building is God's body embracing our life as a community.

In *Listening for the Heartbeat of God*, J. Philip Newell writes of the earth as theophany. He says the fertility of the earth is a sign of how life wells up from within, from the dark unknown place of God. In his homilies on the prologue to St. John's Gospel, Eriugena tells us that God is in all things, the essence of life; God has not created everything out of nothing, but out of his own essence, out of his very life. . . . The world, therefore, Eriugena regarded as theophany, a visible manifestation of God. Even what seems to be without vital movement, like the great rocks of the earth around us, has within it the light of God. To know the Creator, we need only look at the things he has created."[18]

That's why the fascination for us, the ancient of days present in all of it. God greeting us. God making a day of it with us on pilgrimage, driving the countryside in Ireland, or the Highlands in Scotland, or tromping about in fields of scattered stone, and ruin. All of creation exudes God, and is, in and of itself, sacred. The creation rising up and taking shape to reveal God present. And we are in God's presence now, no matter where we are. Listening for God's heartbeat in all of it, like John did when he leaned in to Jesus at the last supper.

***

Initiative for Prayer

Prayer as Object Contemplation

Roll out a piece of wax paper on a table in front of you.

Place some of each of these on the paper: rock, earth, ash, stone, or clay.

What do these make you know about God, about yourself?

What do these make you feel about God, about yourself?

Use your journal to free associate about these questions.

Write a collect using new language for God, from your contemplation experience.

***

In the School of Celtic Consciousness, we practice the listening. I have completed three out of three summer conferences, taught by John Philip Newell, at Mercy by the Sea Retreat and Conference Center, in Connecticut. They gave us certificates, printed on the back of a photo, *Sunrise on Iona*. And they called us scholars.

Practicing the listening, and daring to hear the voice of God, because God is in all of creation. God is as accessible as the ground under your feet and the air in your lungs. So, we listened. Each day, the teachings were punctuated with the spiritual practice of listening, and sometimes visioning.

For one morning's practice, I chose to sit by a butterfly bush, because the purple clusters reminded me of Pennsylvania lilacs. I tried listening to the butterfly, and to the bush that was not a lilac. It was kind of funny to me that what I heard in my listening were my own words from my Easter sermon that former spring, when I quoted my son's scientific poetry about the gigantic promethea moth in his observation box. The chrysalis just hung motionless for weeks like it was vacant. Then unexpectedly one day, it began to shake a bit. And then more. And then nothing again, for more days. And then, shaking again more violently, ever so slowly the gigantic promethea moth with a four-inch wingspan emerged.

He texted me a picture of it, and I asked why it was just hanging there clinging to the cocoon. "Is there something wrong with it?"

That's when he spouted his scientific poetry that stunned my heart. He said it was "unfurling its wings to fly at dusk."

That's when I knew. That's when I understood that mildly troubling resurrection account, when Jesus told Mary not to touch him. I suddenly understood. Mary had walked up on Jesus when he was still wrinkled, and damp, from the effects of having been dead, and the wrapping of linen, and maybe a hundred pounds of spices, bound around his lifeless body for three days. It's no wonder Mary thought that, with such effusive earthiness, surely he was the gardener.

The great silk moth waits there, clinging for a time. Waiting for wings to unfurl, and the venation system of the wings to harden, to give them their structure for flight. A step-by-step primer on resurrection, from entomology. Letting go of the former structure of the chrysalis that no longer contains, or protects, or guards the life within.

Jesus hung around the grave for a bit, waiting for his wings to unfurl. And Mary walked up on him. He was in process, in mid-stream, of resurrection. She showed up early in the morning, while it was still dark, and he wasn't finished yet. That's why she couldn't grab hold, and cling to him, or wrap around his feet when she fell to the ground; he was still unfurling. Mary literally witnessed the Resurrection, while it was happening.

Jesus was still unfurling, still waiting for his skeletal and venous systems to harden, to give his body structure, because resurrection is as much an incarnate experience of the body as was his birth or death. Resurrection, too, is of the earth, and material substance, and is a fully physical event.

How could we abandon or divorce our bodies in death, when we have been born of God? The body is a sacred, precious, inextricable part of us. It is through our bodies, and all material substance, that we know God. Even the creation itself, all the earth, beyond just our own bodies, "groans," as Paul writes in Romans, "in labor pains" for "redemption" (Romans 8:22–23). He says, "the creation itself will be set free from its bondage to decay and will obtain the freedom of the glory of the children of God" (Romans 8:21).

This is the inseparable quality of physical and spiritual existence, which Celtic art so beautifully demonstrates, with intertwined bands, and branches, weavings, Celtic knots, creatures, and even dragons. There is no separation of God and humankind, of God and all creatures, of heaven and earth, of sacred and mundane, of saints, and angels, and our walking the earth. When Esther de Waal writes about Patrick's Lorica, she says:

> It begins with the invocation of the Trinity and then it works its way through all the powers, through angels and archangels, through patriarchs and prophets and apostles, and so to sun and moon, fire, wind, sea, earth and rock, until finally there is each one of us created, surrounded by Christ. It feels as though it is woven in the same way as the Celtic strapwork on the carvings of the high crosses or the intricate pages of decoration of illuminated manuscripts, so that all the elements flow into one strong, gently unified harmony. Here is a powerful sense of the unity of the whole created order, a celebration of creation and redemption, that healing wholeness, the oneness in plurality that has always been so important a gift of the Celtic world.[19]

And there at the bush that was not a lilac on the Long Island Sound, flitted a happy little orange and black butterfly, clinging on to nothing, flying for the sheer pleasure of flight on a light-filled summer morning in Connecticut. Just for the joy of it. This life-over-death kind of resurrection joy.

I was listening for the heartbeat, and what I heard was God's voice in creation inviting me to trust that my own wings have indeed unfurled, already. I heard an invitation to trust my experience of resurrection, and to claim it for myself. My own resurrection, and the brave waiting, clinging to chrysalis, and the process of emergence, and the even braver practice of taking flight, for the delight of resurrection. Simply, for joy. This life-over-death kind of joy, is in the wings. God's body, wing. God's spirit, wind.

Cheers to creation's voice, and God's mercies, which, as the psalmist sings, and the sun confesses, are new every morning. Here's to God's voice in all things, in creation, and in my practice of listening.

I like that they decided to call us scholars rather than graduates. It's an ongoing thing when you're a scholar. We celebrate with graduates because they have finished something and move on to other things. A scholar goes deep, and deeper still, into knowing, listening, practicing, and loving. Celtic consciousness is that mode of being a scholar. A listening scholar.

I recently received an e-mail, and the school is now considering a new name to use for us, rather than scholars. We are now companions. I like it. All of us on a journey together, peregrini out in the world, listening for the heartbeat of God.

Initiative for Prayer

Prayer as Listening for
the Heartbeat of God in Creation

Find a place outside. Position yourself as you see fit. Listen.

Write down what you hear in your journal if you want, or draw, or just be quiet and listen.

PART II

God in Fire

*To include light, bonfire, flame,
spark, ember, hearth, lightning bolt,
firefly, candlestick, spark plug, oil
lamps, hell, campfire, cook stove,
gracious light, and celestial fire.*

Fire is primitive. Essential. Fire is the element that enlivens the other elements. Without fire, air goes dark, water turns hard, earth closes up. Unbreathable air. Undrinkable water. Impenetrable earth. This is the stuff of end-of-the-world science fiction, and the primitive anxiety of the ancients. What if the fire in the sky goes out?

"Kum Ba Yah, my Lord, Kum Ba Yah," a quintessential campfire song and earnest invocation by adolescents for God to come by here. We gather round flame, and crackling ember, and sing for God to visit us. "Come by here." Visit us in this moment, right now with us in this life, where we are. Be here, on this ground, in this fire. Be present, in this place. Fire makes us lean in with an instinctive hunch that something holy, and alive, is happening. We scoot in toward the campfire, maybe we hold hands, or lock arms, perhaps we sway. And if we don't know the Holy One present in the fire, or in the flush of our faces, we know it by the arms we link, and the fire within. Same heat. Same flame. Same effect. God within us, as fire and friend.

The earth's equator tilts. Its axis tips and leans away from the sun. Extreme darkness in the northern hemisphere. Long nights and shortened days, the sun in bits and pieces. Frigid temperatures. The winter solstice. We borrow language to speak of the spiritual crisis of God absent, and the phenomenon we call the dark night of the soul.

Fire is the element that ignites and illumines. Our need for fire is our need for God. Necessity. Our need for fire is our need for life, for food, for heat, and for avoiding a stone-cold death. We need it. We fear it. We want it. We dread it. And so it goes, our fascination, repulsion, attraction, quandary, duplicitous, treacherous, spiritual journey, of life with God, as fire. Finding God, and following God, in holy flame. Our illumination and consummation. We cannot live without it, so we get as close as we can, and try not to get burned.

Celtic spirituality would have us get comfortable and familiar with the handling of the fire. It was for Celtic peoples a way to pray and practice, with ritual, the presence of God in the house, and in the hearth. Praying the day with God in it, in the *smooring* of the fire. Esther de Waal writes of an "artistic and symbolic" ritual that was "performed with loving care" at night, as a woman told it to Alexander Carmichael when he was creating the *Carmina Gadelica*. She told how they would bank down the fire's embers in three parts (for the Trinity) with peat, "So that it would be found alive again the following morning."[20] She shares a smooring prayer from Ireland:

> As I rake the ashes over this fire,
> They are raked by the Son of Mary.
> Blessed be house and fire!
> Blessed be the people under this roof!
> Let an angel stand at the great door,
> Until the ring of day shows in the East.[21]

By changes in the light, we know the time of year, even the time of day. We mark time, and order our days, by changes in the light in an otherwise endless disorder of time and space. Light is our orientation. The sun, our compass rose for finding east, and the general order of the universe by its rising and its going down. The dawn. The dusk. And the nuance of noonday light. We order our prayers for the coming and going of the sun. Our spirituality, like clockwork, orienting our prayer to the play of light, and dark, and fire in the sky. God near, God distant, God gone, God present.

When the sun sets, we sense danger and we pray God to guard. We sense our vulnerability and pray God to "keep watch."[22] We feel our lying down in the dark as we would in the grave, and we pray for the repose of the dead. For God's presence in the night hours, we pray God to "be our companion" and to "kindle our hearts."[23] God, a verb, for our igniting. We pray our ever-desperate need for fire and the presence of God. And for God, to not leave us, but to "be our light in the darkness."[24]

Esther de Waal writes of a Celtic custom among old men to "uncover their heads when they first saw the sun as they came out of the house each morning." A tip of the hat, to "honor the sun as a gift from a God who is the God of light and fire and warmth." Similarly, they would "hail the new moon, 'the great lamp of grace,' with joyous welcome and acclaim." The sun, she says, would be greeted like "a great person come back to their land." These customs and traditions were a way of prayer for a people who lived close to the elements, a holistic Celtic way of praying that issues from "living on this earth" and being "part of the pattern of day and night, darkness and light, the waxing and waning of the moon, the rising and setting of the sun. The whole of myself is inserted into the rhythm of the elements."[25]

The sacred community marks changes in light, liturgically, and creates a whole separate calendar for what spiritual time of year it is, as determined by the coming and going of light.

Advent light is armor for battle. Fighting gear. A tool for foraging and scouring the dark. A weapon for scattering the darkness. And an examining tool for seeking justice.

Epiphany light is God's unveiling. We wait in darkness for light to shine. We search a night sky and follow a star. It stops and stays our journey. Eastern sages usher us in, and Joseph draws back the drape, Mary loosens the swaddling wrap, and we dare to look into the face of God: "the mystery of the Word made flesh." Unveiled. For all the world to see. A "new light to shine in our hearts"[26] and we are illumined. Us—luminaries. The whole of us, full of holy light.

Easter light is "the Morning Star who knows no setting."[27] The first light. Uncreated light. Victorious light that vanquishes death and the grave. Explosive light. Resurrecting light. Paschal fire.

De Waal tells the story of the paschal fire and Patrick of Ireland, a story of God, and only God, as fire and light.

> According to tradition, on Holy Saturday in the year 433 St. Patrick kindled the paschal fire on the hill of Slane which looked across to Tara, the center of the country and the seat of the High-King Laeghaire. The high-king was about to hold a festival in which all the lights and fires in the country were to be extinguished, and then he would light his fire, a ritual proclamation showing that only he and he alone would provide his people with light and fire. St. Patrick's fire was therefore a challenge to his ascendancy, and his wise men warned that unless this rival fire was put out immediately, it would flood the whole country with its light and burn until doomsday.[28]

In Pentecost, light ignites. Tongues of flame, and we are on fire with the compelling indwelling Holy Spirit of God and sent out into the world with missions to accomplish. Empowered by sacred fire. The Holy One as agency, the fuel for the Celtic passion for pilgrimage.

I collected a seed pod on my morning run. Milkweed. A wildly gigantic *Asclepias*, already bursting open with seed, and curvy like a miniature Viking ship. Creation making me know holy truth. God is reaching out to me. The Book of Common Prayer says the creation itself is sacramental. It is God reaching out to us through material things, and the church simply makes patterns of this with material things of choice, like bread, and wine, and water, and oil, to celebrate that God does this all the time; reaches out to us through the material of creation.[29] Every day, in all our days.

Like with my pod. The visible manifesting the invisible, the way the featherweight tuft lifts the seed from its tiny sarcophagus. White silk wings for the wind to convince me of invisible holy presence, and unimaginable promises, and evidence of God's reaching. The Holy One breathing, playing, creating, resurrecting, and sweeping through, but because this is all invisible, I collected this pod. To help me know.

Looking at the pod makes me hear my grandmother's singsong voice reciting the Eugene Field nineteenth-century poem "Wynken, Blynken, and Nod," when I, like the three in the shoe, was a wee one. The first whimsical notion of peregrination, introduced with ease and matter-of-factness, at nursery age. A wooden shoe sailing out in the night lighted by twinkling stars and cheery moon, and in the company of the three. A voyage with the light. My beautiful pod, shaped like a coracle for setting out on pilgrimage with the Holy One. Every Celtic soul, a peregrine, just thrilled at the notion that the journey is worth it, simply, for the love of God. To be out and about in the world, anywhere at all, for the joy and company of the Divine. That's the journey of the day. Of any day. Of this day. To greet the rising of the sun, and set out with jubilation because, wherever my little pod takes me, it is the Holy Spirit in wind, and fire, that puts me out to sea for a sacred journey and holy adventure. The light of Pentecost that empowers us, out into the world. Today is a good day, because it is filled with beautiful, holy presence.

God as fire makes new dangers for us: the possibility of seeing and being seen. The risk of seeing things we've never seen before. The risk of understanding holy mysteries. The risk of being different than we were before we entered that house under the star, or waited in the upper room for unexpected tongues of fire, and the gift of language, and now to be seen by all the world. To be the light of God wherever we go in the world.

Storms rage and the lights flicker. Our power goes out. Matches strike, candles burn, flashlights and lanterns illumine faces. We find a way to hunker down. Come in, come close, and gather round, because suddenly none of us has power. Not even the neighbors. In those moments, when the lights go out, in an inside out sort of way, our households experiment with power. All of us have power because we are equally without it.

A scene on my way to work one morning, passing by a power plant: a cyclone fence surround and a sign posted with red letters in all capitals: DANGER. Two human figures, presumably homeless men, laying on concrete in sleeping bags outside the gate. The juxtaposition was all too obvious and dramatic. Power on the inside of the gate, powerlessness on the outside of the gate. Homelessness, in direct proportion to one's access to power. What does it mean for us to be filled with God as fire, the very power of God for marvelous works, in the face of inequity and inhumanity?

It's a risk to be filled with light. The risk of wielding, and wearing, and possessing light. Light, which the psalmist suggests is the power of God for justice and righteousness (Psalm 37:6 NKJV). Light is that power. Fire is the holy element that moves us from resting in God as position, and place, to adventuring out into the world. Fire makes activists of us all. We are the evidence, and physical manifestation, of the power of God, or as it says in Acts, we are "witnesses" (Acts 1:8), we are first-hand storytellers, because we have first-hand experience of God as fire. And now all the world knows we have it. The world may expect miracles, because we have the power of the Holy Spirit, and the Holy Spirit set us on fire. We are luminaries. We are filled with God and the world knows that we can do something to effect justice.

Fire is an empowering and dangerous element. God in us, the burning of our hearts, the illumination of our minds, the light in our eyes, and the lifting of our countenance. God, "like . . . fire shut up in [our] bones" (Jeremiah 20:9). It's a dangerous thing to go walking around this earth, playing with fire. People expect something. Something powerful, and good, and full of life.

5

DOMESTIC JUSTICE

The winter solstice. All of my people on my father's side are Swedish. The land of the midnight sun and noonday darkness. It's the noonday darkness that I wonder about. I wonder if it is part of me. The moderns wonder if the ancients thought the sun would dip so low that darkness would cover the earth and they would cease to exist. I wonder if it may still be a real possibility. These are my people. Scandinavian. The Swedes. On my father's side, all of them.

I have very few Swedish words and none of them are conversational, just family sayings. I haven't located the domain in Sweden from which we emigrated just yet. But still, my propensity for darkness makes me feel I can claim my ancestral heritage in good faith. And after all, my maiden name is Lindberg, without the h.

I've wondered if one can be genetically predisposed to despair if the Swedes are one's ancestors. All those generations doing battle with darkness, rumors of high suicide rates and depression, would suggest the possibility.

I have lived in darkness. I have been paralyzed by fear, depression, despairing, and altogether waiting for darkness to envelope me and finish me off. Never really expecting light to fill the sky again.

The Advent season takes the stage in the domestic arena. We manufacture darkness. We turn out the lights, and we use a wreath with four candles, and light one at a time over the four weeks before Christmas. It is a mealtime table ritual with household members gathered around.

Our practice is to live a drama. We symbolically join the people of God who have waited in darkness. It is invitation to the dark. To get in it. To name the dark as darkness. To call it what it is. And to pick up battle implements to fight it to the death. We suit up with light as "armor" and we pray God to "stir up his power."[30] Lighting the Advent wreath is a household ritual because that is where we live. And if we live in darkness, the household is dark.

My life is peppered with stories of darkness, all shrouded and shadowed in the cold and dreary place of darkening memory. Some of the work of Advent, and the storytelling about the dark, is provoked externally: seasons change, snow comes, temperatures drop, it gets dark. Or someone dies. Or you are victimized, and exploited, even abused.

None of us, however, chooses where we were born, or of whom, nor do we control the turning of the earth, and the tilting away from the light and warmth of the sun. Nor do we choose to be objectified, victimized, or abused. But what we choose is how we tell the story. The work is internal. It begins there, with a story that illuminates, a story of light and life. It is a story about your choosing, your volition, your dignity, your hope. "In the Celtic tradition . . . redemption is about light being liberated from the heart of creation and from the essence of who we are. It has not been overcome by darkness. Rather, the light is held in terrible bondages within us, waiting to be set free."[31]

You are telling a story when you choose to light a candle and wait for the birth of the Beloved; when you light a candle to be a survivor instead of a victim, to reclaim dignity by assigning responsibility where it belongs, to claim that work as righteousness. You tell a story of light and life where righteousness is right living, right relationship, which is to claim what belongs to you, and make certain what belongs to others.

We make ritual of our storytelling in the dark. One of the stories is that there is a season, or perhaps a whole life, of waiting in darkness, waiting, and watching, and hoping for redemption, salvation, a birth, new life. Advent is the ritual story of choosing light in the darkness. We light the candles. One, then two, three, and four, as an act of empowerment, and change, and a need to do something.

Initiative for Prayer

Prayer as Keeping Vigil with the Moon

Keeping vigil means to be watchful, and to stay, and to keep company. And it inherently involves waiting. This kind of prayer is a practice of watching for or attending the light. This is also a practice of entering the darkness, just as we do in Advent. This practice of vigil will take a month's time, as the simple project is to keep a journal of the phases of the moon.

Divide four journal pages into seven sections each. One for each night of the week for four weeks.

Simply record the changes in the moon. Draw the shape and size of the moon, and note its phase, and note the time, and its position in the night sky. You may want to comment on the moon, your thought or response to it. Or note some other things about the weather or what you've been doing this evening, or anything that strikes your fancy. You may want to research information about the moon or enjoy photography on the internet, but this is completely optional.

Make some journal entries, a page or two for describing your experience of keeping vigil. Make some notes about what was going on externally in your schedule, or work events, or family members and your life together.

How was your process of keeping watch, and waiting, an internal process? How were the nights different throughout the month? How has the experience of darkness changed over this month of keeping vigil?

Prepare the way of the Lord, make his paths straight.
(Luke 3:4)

My car smells delightfully sappy. The Christmas tree farm by the school stacked piles of greens outside the fence, free for the taking, and I stuffed the hatch of my car, full. So even though I was a few days late for the first Sunday in Advent, today we will light two candles at our dinner table. Our wreath is ready. The round circle for the eternity of God with greens for everlasting life, pinecones for fertility and birth, cedar for strength, holly and ivy for immortality, and if I find a piece of laurel somewhere, I'll add it for victory over suffering. Our wreath is ready, and I've got greens galore for mantel and doorways.

"Prepare the way of the Lord, make his paths straight." I know the gospel is describing the ancient way of preparing a road for a royal procession. A king is coming. Of course, I know that. But instead, my head fills with domestic visions, and the seasonal incessant need for making lists. I can't help but translate Isaiah's prophecy about mountains being made low into the mountains of laundry and stacks of dishes instead of gestures of justice.

And the rough and crooked path that needs to be smooth and straight for the king's entourage, becomes, instead, my river-rock sidewalk that doesn't work with my high heels, and makes me walk on my tiptoes while juggling bags of groceries, purse, and briefcase. How do I get ready for a king when I can barely get ready for dinner?

John the Baptist stands in for Isaiah with a message for all the world. Prepare the way. But, really, it gets down to a household parent in a bandana making games of household chores, and swinging brooms, and buckets, and extending ladders.

How do we do Advent, and heed the prophets, and ever get beyond the domestic venue? It seems to me that we don't. Because the holy stuff of Advent is about darkness and light, and birthing God, and those are utterly domestic, and earthy, and immediate.

Darkness and light are as ordinary and immediate as waking and sleeping, and they govern our days, determine our well-being. Advent is about the shortness of days, distance from the sun, and the threat of darkness. The spirituality of Advent is so domestic, and daily, and primitive, that we swiped an ancient custom from pagans and we made a wreath for it.

We mimic pre-Christian cultures to get at what it really is about for us. We follow them, the people who were even more in touch with sun, and moon, and lights in the sky, ancient philosophers, and theologians in their own right. The deep, dark days of winter, light ever diminishing, shrinking before their eyes. In my own ancestral land of Sweden, the sun just skimming the surface of the horizon. And they wonder, would the light go out? Could it? The celestial fire ball, so small and far away, frigid air, frozen ground, barren trees, and earth gone brown. No midnight sun, just noonday darkness. Might the light flicker, and extinguish altogether?

To keep their hope alive, and bear the darkness, they'd take a wheel from the idle carts, and bring it in, and turn it flat on its side. A symbol of stillness and waiting; the quieting of marketplace and machinery. A centering piece decked with evergreens. They would trim wicks, and fire the light, and plead with the god of the sun to come back. We follow them, and defy the power of darkness, with our wheel turned flat on the dining room table. It is our confession that for all our industrious labor, we cannot, after all, sustain light and life. We gather in the darkness. One candle; a second. Three candles; and a fourth. Because what they knew, we know, too. God is an elemental God, God is light and life. And we keep vigil for the light to come among us. And like them, we know the threatening darkness, we know the forces that risk our lives. Our Advent liturgy has us putting on light, "as armor," to do battle with darkness.[32] We wear God for this work, and we become activists to dispel the darkness.

We busy ourselves with outreach and social ministries in Advent. We think we do this because Christmas is a sentimental and joyful season, and we'll have no children without pleasures, no hungry without a feast, no poor without plenty, no lonely without company. But really, we busy ourselves with outreach and social ministries because our king is coming, and we need to hurry up. We need to tidy our house, because we know just enough about this king to know that our house is nothing like his kingdom, and we scramble. We know about this king. We have heard that he champions the widow and orphan, he lifts up the lowly, and crushes the oppressor. He defends the cause of the poor, and gives deliverance to the needy.

We know it. We sing it. His rule is "peace and freedom, and justice, truth, and love."[33] And so we know that in his kingdom there are no children without pleasures, no hungry without a feast, no poor without plenty, no lonely without company. Prepare the way of the Lord, make his paths straight, mountains made low, valleys filled, crooked and rough made straight and smooth. A picture of justice and equity. We feed the hungry, and give to the poor, because in Advent we are trying to bring in the kingdom. We give to the homeless and the needy, because we have become activists for the kingdom of God, and we do justice, where we live, in our schools, and households, and in our neighborhoods, for a domestic kind of spirituality, because Advent is about darkness, and light, and birthing God.

In Advent, we take our place among people who live in darkness waiting for God to come. We're positioning ourselves with people who are desperate to see God's face. We're preoccupied with imagining a king, who wears righteousness for a belt around his waist. We're feeling our way in the dark, and imagining the earth filled with his glory, and we become activists to dispel the darkness. We put on God and wear our armor of light. We watch, and wait, because the King of Kings might be in the near distance. We listen, and we hear tambourines and flutes down the road, and we're sure there's a touch of pink beginning on the horizon. Our hearts pound with excitement. The King is coming. This is his Advent.

Celtic liturgies contained in the *Iona Abbey Worship Book* venture to experiment with commitment services for peace and justice, and articulate what our faith might mean in action. Here is an example of an affirmation of faith with a beautiful call to action.

> We believe that God is present
> in the darkness before dawn,
> in the waiting and uncertainty
> where fear and courage join hands,
> conflict and caring link arms,
> and the sun rises over barbed wire.
> We believe in a with-us God
> who sits down in our midst to share our humanity.
> We affirm a faith that takes us beyond the safe place
> into action, into vulnerability,
> and into the streets.
> We commit ourselves to work for change,
> and put ourselves on the line,
> to bear responsibility, take risks,
> live powerfully and face humiliation;
> to stand with those on the edge,
> to choose life
> and be used by the Spirit
> for God's new community of hope.
> Amen.[34]

We know how to make our way in the dark because we have our wreath. We wind our way into the very center, the deepest darkness, the winter solstice of the soul, and there, the light of Christ burns bright, just as the light of Christ burns in the very center of our being. In *Listening for the*

Heartbeat of God, J. Philip Newell writes about the ninth-century philosopher John Scotus Eriugena, a teacher in the Celtic church.

> In his homilies on the prologue to St John's Gospel, Eriugena tells us that God is in all things, the essence of life; God has not created everything out of nothing, but out of his own essence, out of his very life. This is the light that is in all things. . . . The world, therefore, Eriugena regarded as theophany, a visible manifestation of God.[35]

While we know the threatening forces of darkness, we also know that "when earth stood hard as iron, water like a stone,"[36] the light that brightens sun, and moon, and stars in the night sky, became flesh and dwelt among us. "Light shines in the darkness, and the darkness did not overcome it" (John 1:5).

Initiative for Prayer

Prayer as Singing the Light, Ancient Voice and Common Prayer

The *Phos hilaron* is an ancient prayer of the church and is found in the rite for Evening Prayer.[37] The Latin title means "happy light," the English title is "O Gracious Light." Use this prayer daily, for a week.

Open yourself to being sensitive to the light, and watch, and wait for the light to change toward evening. Notice it. Just at the point when you notice the change in light from day to night, at eventide, sing God's praise with this prayer. Say the prayer out loud, have others join you if there are others around. Try singing the prayer using one of the hymn tunes in *The Hymnal 1982.*

Know that when you pray this prayer, people the world over are praying it with you since it is in the Daily Office for evening. Enjoy the company of the saints.

Know, too, that you are experimenting with names and images for God, because in this prayer we call God "O Gracious Light." God is this light, and we are singing his praises. There is no darkness that can overcome this light.

O Gracious Light—*Phos hilaron*

O gracious Light,

pure brightness of the everliving Father in heaven,

O Jesus Christ, holy and blessed!

Now as we come to the setting of the sun,

and our eyes behold the vesper light,

we sing your praises, O God: Father, Son, and Holy Spirit.

You are worthy at all times to be praised by happy voices,

O Son of God, O Giver of life,

and to be glorified through all the worlds.[38]

———————

6

WHO ARE YOU?

Who are you? Who am I?

To some extent I can answer that question by saying who I am not. I am not you. I am not a man. I am not a youth. I am not a mathematician. Our never-ending quest to understand our existence, and the nature of our being, and exactly who we are. And how to answer the question: who are you?

My daughter Caroline is driving off for a holiday weekend. She is my little mile marker for my life as a priest. I was pregnant with her when I was ordained, and now she is twenty-seven years old. Her due date was on June 4, my ordination was scheduled for June 6, and she was born on June 11.

I am a mother. I am a priest.

Are motherhood and priesthood about identity, and being, as in, "This is who I am," or are they roles that I fulfill, as in, "This is what I do"? Seven of us were ordained together at the Cathedral of St. Philip. My ordaining bishop quipped about my unborn child during the ordination service, and what her identity would be in the church. He suggested that the theologians are still out on the subject, on the theology of ordination. In the theological debate, one argument is that ordination confers an office on a person, and that the priest functions as a sacrament and symbol-bearer for the church. Others argue that ordination is ontological, and has to do with being, and that with the laying on of hands a person's being changes, and the person becomes a priest, or in other words is changed, and made into a priest by the ordination. "So," he said, "it is still in question about this unborn baby; if the ontological argument wins out, it will mean that with the laying on of hands, this baby, too, will be ordained."

Caroline and I have enjoyed our little secret society over the years of her life, like two peas in a pod. Actually, she was the pea; I was the pod. She is a very knowing person, intuitive, observant, compassionate, insightful, and a natural celebrant. She is, through and through, an instinctive caregiver, the one to tend her grandpa's gashed shin, the one to tuck her grandmother in her seatbelt, the one to join her step-grandmother as a necessary companion on a long journey to tend, the one to comfort with affection; she, a nurturer, and servant, a helper, with a naturally endowed priestly quality we call pastoral. Her penchant for celebration is over the moon with effusive joy and scrupulous detail. Every person to be recommended for holy orders should be tested as to whether or not they like to throw a party, because that is what we do, every Sunday, and she was born for it. The priest is the celebrant and throws a party, one so bountiful that we call it the Eucharistic Feast. And besides all that she is also organized, and gifted in administration, a necessary quality that makes most clergy agonize. Whether she was literally ordained in my belly or not, she is a priest in her own right, as much a priest as anyone I have ever known. She is the package deal. Which begs the question: Does the church recognize the priest in a person, and ordain them to it, or does the church make a priest, by the act of ordaining?

Nearly four years earlier, the same bishop got news, by way of the report from my psychological examination, that I was pregnant with my first child. I was enrolled in the Vocational Testing Program, the pre-seminary year of exploration and examination that was a diocesan requirement and the singular avenue by which one can be recommended for holy orders. The Canon to the Ordinary, who is the bishop's right-hand person, called me on the phone one afternoon. She said she thought I should withdraw from the program. She thought I should go have the baby and then I would know, after I became a mother, whether or not I really wanted to also become a priest.

I was appalled. Indignant. And terribly disappointed. I was thirty-two years old and had worked in the church professionally for seven years. I thought I had done enough watching, waiting, exploring, and testing to know for certain that priesthood was the direction for my life.

I told her I did not intend to withdraw, and asked what I could do to stay in the program. She told me I would have to defend my cause. After further questioning, examination, conversations, conferences, letter-writing, therapists, they said, with a big sigh, "Well okay, against our better judgment, you can stay in the program." David was born over our Christmas break, and went everywhere with me, cradled and swaddled, nursing and napping, and we were in it together. I was recommended for holy orders at the end of the program, and started seminary the following fall, when he was eight months old. I still have the letters justifying my cause, but I don't read them. I'm not even sure where they are.

The only thing that I remember saying in my defense was that priesthood and motherhood, for me, were of a piece. Two strands of one cord, each wrapped in, and around, and through the other. I've rarely felt certain about anything, but about these I was sure: becoming a mother and becoming a priest. Pursuing both at the same time made perfect sense to me, partly because of a simple timing issue. I was concerned that at my age, if I became a priest first, I might never get on in time to having children. If I became a mother first, I might be constrained in such a way as to never make it back to school, seminary no less, to complete a three-year master's degree program.

But besides the logic, and convenience, of pairing the two in the same season of my life, these were two things I knew about myself, about who I am. My internal self confirmed my identity with nodding; my knowing was a "yes." Determination. Certainty. It was time. Birth certificates, ordination certificates, blood, sweat, and tears for all of them. And scars.

The bishop dripped melting wax on my ordination certificate, sealed it with his ring, and signed his name. I framed it. Now, it takes its place in the attic like an archive. Do the certificates tell me who I am? Do they make me who I am? Do they tell the world what the world needs to know about me? Is that why clergy hang certificates on their office walls—because we don't otherwise know that we were born, or that we are priests? Is this how I know who I am? Is this, who I am, an ordained priest, or is this, what I do, practice my priesthood? Am I a mother, or do I mother? Mother and Priest. Priest and Mother.

Awkwardly, people ask, "What should we call you?" It's another way of saying they don't know what I am, or what to make of me. They don't mind that "Reverend Ruth" is grammatically incorrect as a spoken address; they say it anyway. It is intended to be a written title, after the word "The." They would rather not say "Mother Ruth." And they feel it's not proper to allow their children to just say "Ruth," so they call me "Reverend Ruth."

Liturgically, when we welcome the newly baptized, one of the things we say as a congregation is, "Share with us in his eternal priesthood."[39] We say it to babes in arms. We are, all of us, priests. I am a priest, among priests, in a community of priests.

When I lead a baptism seminar, I hold up two white garments. One, the linen gown my own children wore when they were baptized; the other, the cassock alb, the white garment that a priest wears over street clothes and under other vestments. I tell these parents that I am a priest by virtue of my baptism, and that they will be raising a priest in their household. The anointed one. The beloved of God in their midst; and they themselves as parents are the face of God by which their children will know the love of God, or not. I tell the gathered worshiping community that I wear a collar as a sign and symbol. A sacramental gesture, the outward and visible, to remind them, not of my call to priesthood, but of theirs. They are called by God. God says their names in the still of the night just as he said "Samuel," over, and over, until Samuel finally said, "Speak, for your servant is listening" (1 Samuel 3:10). Sometimes it takes some getting used to, to hear and recognize the voice of God calling our names.

Ontology is a branch of philosophy that considers our existence, our being. The essence of who we are. Does the church recognize a person's essence by the act of ordination, or does the church change essence and make a priest by the act of ordination? What of priesthood is about existence and being? What am I? How am I a priest or mother? In other words, what qualities of me are "priest" and "mother"? How much of me? And where am I a priest or mother, in my relatedness to others?

The water of baptism is an outward and visible sign, a ritual gesture of all sorts of things: spiritual truths about freedom, and liberation, being born, initiation into a community, cleansing, victory over death, and resurrection, creation, and re-creation. Perhaps it could be said that the water is a sign of essence and being, getting at the truth of who we are, and how it is that God is within and through us, and what we are together as a people of God. Celtic wisdom holds that the essential goodness of creation still resides at the center of our being, and that our souls, and bodies, through and through, are sacred.

In *Christ of the Celts*, Newell recalls the teachings of an early church father, Irenaeus of Lyons of the second century, just one teacher removed from Jesus's disciple John, who penned the gospel, three letters, and the book of Revelation. Polycarp was a student of John, and Irenaeus was a student of Polycarp.

> So Irenaeus speaks of creation coming out of the very "substance" of God. It is not as if the elements of the universe are fashioned out of a neutral substance. It is not as if creation is set in motion from afar. The matter of life comes forth directly from the womb of God's being. The glory of the sun rising in the east is the glory of God shining on us now and now and now. The whiteness of the moon, the wildness of the wind, the moisture of the fecund earth is the glow and wildness and moistness of God now. It is the very stuff of God's being of which we and creation are composed.[40]

Ontology. Our never-ending quest to understand our existence, and the nature of our being, and who it is, exactly, that we are. And how to answer the question, "Who are you?" It's no wonder that people, from John the Baptist to Caesar Augustus, wanted to know the same from Jesus: "Who are you?" It's no wonder that my bishop wondered who, and what, my child would be. It's no wonder that people ask me all the time, when they see me in clergy garb, "What are you?" I am a mother. I am a priest. I am the baptized. I am the substance of God, in the form of Ruth.

Initiative for Prayer

Prayer as Calligraphy and Puzzling

Find a piece of high-quality letter writing paper or art paper. Write your first name in fancy script, in your own personal style of calligraphy. Use colors if you like, or just ink pen.

Sit with your name and wonder about who you are. Say it out loud, sing it, whisper it, call it out like you're trying to get your own attention. Say it playfully like someone whose accent is different from yours. Sit silently with your name and wonder at it, listen to it. Ask your name to tell you what it means.

Add flourishes to the calligraphy if you're inspired by what you heard. Write your name on another piece of paper in block letter printing. For each letter of your name, write out a word that describes you or says something about who you are, in the style of a crossword puzzle. Now write a clue, as you would in a crossword puzzle, for each letter of your name. If it resonates with you, make more crossing over words that speak to your ontology as you understand it, along with the questions or clues that hint at these words.

Initiative for Prayer

Prayer as Self-Portrait

Draw a loosey-goosey picture of yourself, head and shoulders, without trying to make a look-alike, not an exact replica, just an approximation. With generous abstract brush strokes, with acrylic paint, watercolors, temperas, or even crayons, color yourself in with atypical colors for skin, hair, and features. Now cut three small, curved pieces out of construction paper or magazine scraps, small enough that the three together make a circle slightly larger than your head. Now cut three small straight pieces out of the same paper.

Glue or paste these pieces into a tri-radial nimbus, around your head. A tri-radial nimbus is a halo, divided into three sections by the straight radial pieces, to signify the Holy One, the Sacred, the Divinity, in art.

Spend some time with your abstract self-portrait, and contemplate the Celtic notion that the essential goodness, and the sacred essence, resides in you, as it did in the creation of the world in Genesis 1. If you like, scribble these words like a nameplate at the base of your collage: Darkness has not overcome the Light.

But when Herod heard of it, he said, "John, whom I beheaded, has been raised." (Mark 6:16)

Mark takes the extreme drama in a high-end narrative and spins it as a haunting. The memory of a king, from a night with his queen. A royal banquet for courtiers, and officers, gone frightfully bad. The party, and the players, shifting with deliberated chessboard strategy, vengeance, and vendetta, crossed and double-crossed, check and checkmate. An evening of intoxicating drink, and dance, beaded skirts, and flourishes, wishes, and fancies, taking a razor's edge of demands, and commands, and in the end a beheading.

A final procession through the great hall to present: John the Baptist's head, on a platter. A frenzied crowd, and a sorrowful king, muttering, "That's not what I meant to do." A whisper, and upon the breathing of it, John's words bang in Herod's head. He remembered John saying something about a baptism of repentance. And there in a bigger-than-life haunting, Herod is sure that Jesus is John, back from the dead.

A story with all the gospel ingredients about repentance and the dead raised, but twisted up and inside out with guilt and dread. "John whom I beheaded has been raised." John, animating Jesus? Or Jesus, John? Who's who and which is which?

Their lives inextricably bound, the two of them. Jesus and John, their stories wound around each other woven in and through. Their mothers sang songs and circled about their birth stories. Both with womb secrets: fertile and barren; too young and too old. Mary and Elizabeth with divine love, and a telling of their boys, the cousins, brothers, prophets, sons.

Jesus and John, each a foil for the other, reflecting the one you want to see by showing himself as something different from the other. I am not the light. John constantly telling about who Jesus is by saying who he, himself, is not. Light, not light. Messiah, not messiah. Worthy, not worthy. The message and the messenger. One, a voice in the wilderness. The other, the Word. One, the Way. The other, preparing it.

The two of them get in the river together. The baptized and the baptizer in the water. Visions, and voices from heaven, and a brief behind-the-scenes conversation about who should baptize whom. John baptizes Jesus and both get wet in the River Jordan. One feasts with sinners and prostitutes, the other subsides on locusts and wild honey. One, a glutton by religious standards; the other, holy and righteous. One with a baptism of water and repentance, promising that the other will immerse in fire and Holy Spirit.

There is one, who comes after me, one, more powerful than me. He wears sandals and I am not worthy to untie them. And yet, a prostitute with unbundled hair will weep, and wash his blessed baptized feet, again, with her tears. Hair shirt and leather belt, or seamless tunic put to a gamble? Which is which? A veritable who's who in Bible trivia.

Are you the one? No. Are you the one? And Herod doesn't know. The ever-burning question of the day for Jesus is "Who are you?" And to Jesus, in Mark 6, Herod asks, are you John the Baptist raised from the dead? Are you one and the same? There is Herod, brooding over his bloodbath, riddled with grief, haunted by despair and the mess of his life. Forlorn, and missing it altogether, certain in his confusion that John the Baptist is all there is. Judgment. Condemnation, and himself a viper among a brood of vipers, fleeing the wrath to come (Matthew 3:7).

Before the dreadful night of his beheading, while John waited in Herod's prison, John sent his own question to Jesus: Are you the one? I am not the light, are you? Are you the Messiah, that I was not? Are you the one more powerful than me? Do you bring fire and Holy Spirit? Are you the one to come after me, or should we keep waiting (Matthew 11:3)?

Jesus sent word back to John: "Tell John what you hear and see: the blind receive their sight, the lame walk, the lepers are cleansed, the deaf hear, the dead are raised, and the poor have good news brought to them" (Matthew 11:4–5). John would know what Jesus meant, because John knew that his own baptism of repentance wasn't enough. He waited for the one who would bring fire and Holy Spirit. John would know, you can't grow new limbs with spiritual discipline, and yet the lame leap. John would know, you can't wash yourself clean with the water of repentance, and yet lepers are cleansed. You can't lift yourself out of the grave, pull yourself with dust and ashes all over you, out of despair, and desolation, and yet the dead are raised.

John would know all of this, because John knew that John the Baptist was not all there is. There is this one, Jesus. Light in the darkness. A Way in the wilderness. The Holy Beloved One swirling, and twirling about in you, animating your flesh and blood, with fire in your bones, and the quickness in your breath. Fire, and Holy Spirit, animating you all over again. "The Celtic mission . . . in line with the mysticism of St John, emphasized the truth that God is the 'light of life.' Repentance, therefore, was a turning to what is most deeply planted within us, the light that has not been overcome by the darkness."[41]

The person of Jesus is not just skin around the haunting words of John the Baptist. But he is one who is altogether different. Jesus does not condemn the world, he saves the world. Jesus does not prepare us for God, he is God in us. The Good News is not judgment and condemnation, like the Baptism of John and the water of repentance. The Good News is Jesus. Himself. The Good News is not a message saying: "change your life," "live a different way." It is about being. Be healed. Be whole. Be filled with fire, and Holy Spirit. Be new, a new creature altogether. Wholly, utterly, undeniably new. Ontology, and the shockingly good news about who you are. The Good News is not about how to patch, and repair, this despairing haunted life.

Jesus is light, and life, and a way in the wilderness. Jesus comes with fire and Holy Spirit, to awaken the divine light that resides in us from the foundation of the world.

Initiative for Prayer

Prayer as Collage in a Three-Part Process

Part One

As an act of prayer, create this collage:

Collect pictures, or copies of pictures, of yourself. Use recent pictures or pictures from all different stages of your life. Print or write these phrases on strips of paper:

- The Baptized
- The Beloved of God
- Anointed One
- Child of the Most High God
- Habitat for Holy Spirit
- Image of Divine Love
- Priest in a Kingdom of Priests

Attach the phrases haphazardly with the photos on a poster board.

Part Two

As a practice of prayer, meditate on this poster for ten minutes a day for seven days.

Don't direct your thoughts, just look. If it makes you feel more like you are praying, you can sit cross-legged on the floor with your hands on your knees, palms up. Or post it on the wall where you get ready in the morning; or above the stove, sink, or spice rack. Or strap it in the seatbelt of your back seat while you drive around town as a gesture of precious tending.

Part Three

As a ritual act of celebration, jot down thoughts on a journal page at the end of the seven days. Liturgically, the priest is the celebrant and lifts up substance to say to the community, "God is in this." So here, you are the celebrant, in your own life. Lift your poster up and make the proclamation, "God is in this," or "God is in the substance that is me."

Consider what you experienced this week. No right answers; this is prayer.

Were you inspired? Did you feel silly or embarrassed, or did you wonder if the week would ever end? How do you feel about yourself? How did it make you feel in general? Or about God? Did you have any moments of healing, or joy, or delight? Any new insights, or stirred memories?

7

INVITATION TO PLAY

The Easter Vigil service with baptism and the possibility of nine biblical readings can last for an eternity. So, we debate in staff meetings, do we give the children vigil candles, or just their parents? Or maybe, some would suggest, we get little battery candles, or glow sticks just for the effect of firelight? Drives me nuts.

Vigil candles are for keeping vigil. For keeping watch and making ready. Vigil candles, for each of us. Our tiny resurrected light right there in our hands for our grasping, our flickering hope of God in the grave to bring us out again. Vigil candles, lighted from the Great Paschal Candle that is the Christ, who is just right now in this moment of the drama, vanquishing death. Our own little lighted wick of the new uncreated fire of Resurrection. All of this and our main concern is safety? I don't know. Would it be so bad if resurrection burns a little? A dear old man priest friend of mine torched his vestments a couple of years ago, but the ever-ready eucharistic minister next to him stomped it out with her prayer book. Speedy quick, like she had been commissioned as the fire marshal all along.

My David, when he was in the height of his boyhood years, passed me a little wax cross over the rail when he came up for communion. He had melted down his whole candle and molded the warm wax. The glory of contemplation, and meditation. Monks have nothing on him. Prayer is just that, the contemplation of fire, which is to say, the want of it. The awe, the fascination, the compelling drawing near. A want for the heat. The light. The sense of presence that it creates. A want for God in holy fire.

Holy fire makes us think of purity, and purification, and the irreconcilable tension of what we think we must lose in order to gain God. The insufferable damage that we fear we might incur. The Bible is full of grizzly and primitive notions of the accepted wisdom that God wants to destroy us. Hellfire and brimstone preachers of the Great Awakening ramped it up to such fury that even by my 1960s childhood, the fire still raged. I was terrorized by the same kind of preaching that said: be afraid of God, because you are worthy of destroying.

One time, Benno was putting his boy to bed when he was little and used a leftover vigil candle for their night prayers. His boy kept playing with the flame. Touching, shadowing, swiping at it; blowing, and making it dance. Catching the dripping wax. He was distracted by it. Which, I think, is the point. Not distracted from prayers but attracted to God. And that is prayer: a simple candle with a flame, and letting the fire have its way with us.

Young children haven't heeded our warnings yet, they just get caught up in the flickering presence. Their remedy is dance. Purification through holy dance, barefoot dancing around the flame, exultation in the Gracious Light. Holy Fire as invitation to play. To let our distraction be our attraction, to swipe, and shadow, and see how close we can get to the mesmerizing beauty of the Holy One in fire. And to make our prints in the melting wax, and risk our getting burned.

I want the fire. I want the play. The dance. The heat. The flame. The melting wax. The holy light. The invitation to holy fire and grasping God because I want to be alive. And I do not want to be afraid.

Nine of us gathered before the break of dawn. The word "gathered" is a bit of a stretch. Rummaged really. We rummaged around in the dark. It is the spiritual life, this rummaging around in the dark, and the spirituality of Holy Week and Easter. Our rummaging. The darkness. A veritable ransacking if you think about it. Darkness and lostness. And fighting sleep. All symbols of death. Disciples who were heavy with the pull of gravity, and the grave, such that they could not stay awake in the garden with Jesus. Could not pull themselves out, for knowing themselves to be going down into the deep.

The story says that the women came to the tomb while it was still dark. Sounds like more rummaging to me. We want to feel it in our bones, know it in the fiber of our being, so there we are in the dark, tromping around in wet grass, bundled for cold in the wee hours of Easter morning. We imagine ourselves to be nearing the edge of the tomb, though a simple cold fire pit is what it actually is. We stumble around, and can't find our stuff, and whisper, even though it doesn't matter if anyone hears us; it's the instinctive behavior of operating in the dark, or when something precious and holy is underway. Brave birdsong not minding to wake up the world.

We act things out. That's what ritual is about. We do it so we know it. We act things out, not the full extent of the drama, but in symbol, and gesture, we act it out. We kindle new fire. The cold dark empty echoing fire pit bursts into flame, and we say, "The Light of Christ" and "Grant that in this Paschal feast, we may so burn."[42]

The ancient church gave us a pillar candle, weighty and worthy of leading the lot of us in procession for the whole of Easter season; it's their instinct that fire is the stuff of resurrection and that we should carry it around. The implement. The element. The power. An outward, and visible, sign of the divine fire ablaze in our souls, that enlivens us, as if we are fresh from the grave. The uncreated light that fuels the life of the world. So, we kindle. New fire. And it is the Christ for us, risen from the dead.

Children intuitively see God in the lighting of wicks, and, in fact, their inclination is to play with the flame. Our inclination is to say, "Be careful, you might get burned." Well? I think the nearness of God does burn, and I suspect that the resurrection will singe quite extensively, and I can't help but remember that story where the Holy Spirit lighted up an upper room, caught their hair on fire, and everybody spoke in different languages. What a hoot. God in holy fire was playing with them. Practicing the Resurrection is our taking up God's invitation to play. And yes, with fire. We play with fire. This Holy Uncreated Light. Rummaging around in the dark, and practicing resurrection.

In the Easter season we lead the procession with the Paschal candle, that tall pillar candle that we lit with the flame of the new fire before daybreak. And we light our tall thin beeswax votives. Our procession of resurrection. Our ritual play. We act it out. We want to feel it in our bones, know it in the fiber of our being. Flickering candles that compel us because of the flame, even if sometimes it seems just a preoccupation with the fire itself. That preoccupation is a good thing; it is the presence of God with and within us. Be preoccupied with the fire, and God in it. Recognize the fire as God, name it as the light of Christ that is within you. Grab hold of it, and carry it as your passion for God, your delight in the Holy One, your mirror reflecting the fire of your own resurrected life, and everlasting light. Feel the heat and melting wax as tangible evidence of what is true in and for you. This is our rummaging around in the dark for God, and bursting into flame with his resurrection. Lighting a simple candle for death's vanquishing.

———

Initiative for Prayer

Prayer as Rummaging Around in the Dark

Add a votive candle or a taper to your oratory. And some matches. Find a dark place and sit quietly. Ready yourself in anticipation of God's rising from the dead. Rummage around in the dark for the candle in your oratory. When you find it, whisper a little with thoughts of vigil. Light the candle and say something like "The Light of Christ" and "Grant that in this Paschal feast we may so burn."[43]

———

Initiative for Prayer

Prayer as Presence and Memory

In a relaxed moment when you have the luxury of time and staying power, build a fire in the fireplace, or campfire setting, or in a charcoal pit in the back yard. Gather around with family or friends and allow the conversation to evolve. Listen to the stories people tell. See what happens to come to mind for each person. There may be new stories from the day or the past week. People might tell stories that start with something like "remember when we . . ." Make a mental note of the mood of the stories and where the stories come from in your shared history.

All of these memories are present to God: the people you recall from years ago, and the events that we conjure up to talk about. Remember this is how prayer and storytelling can provide the healing of memories. If some of the stories are about people who have died, remember that they are alive in God, and are there with you in the remembrances, and sit with you at the fire. Another option for storytelling is to literally read stories. Use story books to fuel the imagination.

Consider taking off your shoes and dancing around the holy flame since you are on holy ground, warming at the presence of God in fire, and in the presence of the Divine in all things.

For we have been sold, I and my people, to be destroyed, to be killed, and to be annihilated. (Esther 7:4)

If your hand causes you to stumble, cut it off; it is better for you to enter life maimed than to have two hands and to go to hell, to the unquenchable fire." (Mark 9:43)

A blaze that carries both warning about the flame and invitation to the heat. Firelight that entices us to tell stories, and sing songs, and wonder about life. Our primitive fascination with fire beckons us to gather round it.

God in fire, and water, earth, and air. God of creation, an elemental God who inhabits matter to make himself known. And now Jesus takes up talk about fire. And we pull in close to the flame. And we begin to wonder about God, and the fire of God, and holiness, and purity. And we begin to remember our sacred stories, and we tell them to each other, again and again.

Moses barefoot, to dance on holy ground. Fire in a bush, and it is not consumed. The Holy One has come to speak his name, out of the flame. A pillar of fire by night in the wilderness journey, the presence of God keeping company in their lost-ness, by fire. Flickering fire moving in the night sky to lead sages to the Christ Child born in Bethlehem. The Holy Spirit on each disciple, and it looks like fire, as in exotic stained-glass windows for Pentecost, red, orange, and leaping, tongues of fire.

We gather around the fire, and we begin to wonder about God, and holy mysteries, and holy fire, and eventually we work our way around to wondering if the fire could extinguish us. The age-old wondering. Will God destroy us?

And so, there is this fiery valley outside the gates of Jerusalem that burns all the time. A valley with its own destructive heat, and self-sustaining flame. And Jesus mentions it out loud. A place called "Gehenna" (Mark 9:43, footnote), otherwise translated into English as "hell." It has become the very depiction of punishment. The punishment of God.

Hellfire. Damnation. Brimstone. A valley that lies in wait, a taunting threat outside the gates, and the possibility of extinction.

This valley called Gehenna is a place in Israel where generations before, religious ritual took the form of infant sacrifice—babies offered up to consuming flames. Offspring, annihilated with fire. Heritage and identity, scattered in ash to the wind. Progeny, destroyed. Life snuffed out at their own hands, toying with their own genocide, tempting fate with a mock-play of extinction. Offering up their little ones and daring the gods to answer, "Will you destroy us?"

We gather around the fire and wonder about God. And with the fire comes a sense of dread. What about Holy Fire? Will God destroy us? And what might we sacrifice to prevent it, because it makes us afraid? And with this fiery valley as the backdrop, Jesus mentions, our little ones, and our faith community, and how we put stumbling blocks in front of the little ones who believe in him, already.

What do we do that preserves this faith in a little one, or destroys it in sacrifice? Those stumbling blocks. There is a suggestion implicit in what Jesus says, that if stumbling blocks are removed, these little ones are the very ones who know their way with God. Babies and children, God-ward from the beginning. Born to make their way, if unrestrained, unobstructed. Do not trip them. Do not prevent them. Do not sacrifice them, to work out your own religion. Open the gate. Clear the way, for the little ones who would otherwise sing, and dance, and play their way to the Divine, if not for the falling over the stumbling blocks that we put in front of them.

Stumbling blocks. Guilt. Debt and obligation. Superstitions. Social structures. Conformity. Hatred and injustice. Lists and demands. To name just a few. Us with our stumbling blocks constructing a kind of genocide for God. We hand down all our religious anxieties, which do indeed prevent them. If we prevent them, the rest of us, Jesus says, might as well drop to the bottom of the sea, because the little ones are the ones who know how to get there. To God. And we need them to take us.

Furthermore, Jesus says, "What about you? Why are you afraid?" For all our modernity, high tech, and high finance, high culture, and ultra-communications, we are really rather primitive, because we are afraid. We are afraid the Holy Fire will destroy us. Jesus suggests we are our own extinction. Throwing our whole selves to destruction because we grab hold to what really doesn't matter.

Look at the fiery valley outside the city gates and tell the truth of it. What pulls you into it, and what makes you think you will burn there forever? What threatens to be your end, your extermination? What threatens to annihilate you and snuff out your life?

Newell turns to the teachings of Eriugena for the explanation of how evil persists, when Celtic spirituality so relentlessly endorses the goodness of creation and the light within us, which darkness has not overcome.

> The Celtic tradition is led to affirm that the goodness of God is at the very heart and inception of all life. "The Divine Goodness," as Eriugena says, "summons all things out of not-being into being." This is not to be naïve to the ways in which creation is blighted and diseased. . . . Despite this the Celtic tradition has celebrated the goodness that is deeper than evil . . . [and] define[s] evil as essentially destructive. . . . The momentum of evil is always towards non-being and meaninglessness. The degree to which any created thing becomes evil is the extent to which it ceases to truly exist. It becomes false to itself.[44]

The feminine voice of a queen echoes behind that story about Gehenna in the ninth chapter of Mark's gospel. The wistful woe in Esther's telling, "We have been sold." Slavery. Purchased people. "We have been sold, I and my people, to be destroyed, to be killed, and to be annihilated" (Esther 7:4). At risk of extinction. Her story, a captivity chronicle of how a whole people could be lost. No memory of their existence. No trace. No generations. Their treasure trove of stories about how it is that we are saved, all lost to the world. Collections. Annals. Poems and songs. Divine love stories, and ballads of the beloved, cease to exist. Feasts and festivals, dancing processions for the joy of the Lord. All on the auction block, to be silenced on the gallows.

Esther is, herself, an unknown woman in a harem of women. Her own story already seeping away, her Persian king, her royal husband, doesn't even know she is a Hebrew woman. On the eve of the gallows her people prepared for hanging, a thorough extermination of lineage on the morrow, she found her voice, and said the freeing truth of her story: "We have been sold, I and my people, to be destroyed, to be killed, and to be annihilated." The possibility of extinction, and the truth of her story proclaimed.

What is the truth of it for you? What is your truth? Tell it. What threatens to be your end, your annihilation? Whatever it is, hack and gouge for the truth of your story, and set yourself free. Cut it off. Dig it out. Yank it up by the roots. Guilt. Debt. Obligation. Superstitions. Social structures. Hatred. Shame. Conformity. Lists. Demands. Family legend. Disappointment. Jealousy. These stumbling blocks we carry around. Use a chisel if you need one. Get down to bone and clay. Deep inside of you is holy substance. It's nothing in comparison to losing the life it robs from you. Do the grizzly work, and lop it off. Limp a little until you learn to walk differently. Free yourself of whatever threatens to consume you, to be your end, to annihilate you, and to extinguish life for you.

It's a primitive thing to do, but we are disturbed with primitive anxieties. We are afraid. Fire and flood, slavery and bondage, captivity and exile. Cut yourself loose. Let the Divine Goodness in you call your non-being into being.

Use the fire of God to rid and purify. Throw it in and be done with it. Test the Holy Fire. Ask the primitive questions that never go away. Will the fire destroy me? Or might the fire already inhabit me?

Do what the children do. Sing songs, make poems, rhyme rhymes. Play with fire. Dance your way to the Divine. Get in close, take off your shoes, and dance a holy dance around the Holy Fire.

Initiative for Prayer

Prayer as Making Fire and Household Ritual

Obtain a flint used for making fire. Check with a Boy or Girl Scout who might be able to provide one, or check with outfitters and camping stores. Explore the invoking of God, the invitation to God, to "come by here" in fire. Begin a new fire whose flame is not from another fire, but is uncreated, in the way that we practice at Easter vigil, by striking flint. Enjoy the challenge of making the fire.

Hint: dryer lint catches the flame very easily, and of course very slim pieces of kindling would come next. Enjoy the fire itself for a time before moving to the next step.

Option 1. Repentance

With paper and pencil, jot down ways in which your hands, and feet, and eyes have caused you to stumble. Tear these into individual strips. Collect the pile of papers in your hands. Offer thanksgiving prayers for the essence of the holy child within you, who is still full of the light of God, and dances and plays at the center of your soul, in communion with the Holy Fire of God. Without these stumbling blocks to prohibit you, invite your inner child to the new freedom of being stumbling-block free, and toss the papers into the flame.

Option 2. Holy Fire on Household Pilgrimage

Light seven new votive candles, or just one for each participant, from the fire and take them into the darkened house. Walk them through the house together, into each room, to dispel the darkness. In each room say this call and response:

Leader: Light shines in the darkness.

Response: And the darkness has not overcome it.

Before you leave each room, turn on the lights and leave them burning.

Now place the candles in the dish of sand on the dinner table together to enjoy the firelight, and bring out some bread and wine or other treats for an impromptu feast.

―――――

8

BARE FEET

Sometimes I preach barefoot. The pulpit was solid wood at St. Thomas and gave me cover. As it was, I already stood on a carpeted Coke crate turned upside down, the old wooden kind that carried twenty-four glass bottles. I'm five feet and one inch tall, and pulpits were designed for men. Altars too, and vestments. The black shirt and backwards collar, all masculine construction. I am a woman of feminine stature in a man's profession, so I make adjustments—safety pins, duct tape, and Coca-Cola crates flipped over.

My female colleagues often yield their feminine costuming to the masculine images in church supply catalogues, or the former rectors' gallery on the parish hall wall, or the ones archived in their childhood memories. They surrender to the khaki gaberdine skirt or black trousers to go with the black shirt, then throw on some very ordinary thick-soled, cushioned, trip-averse shoe to complete the outfit that apologizes for being woman. A woman, trying to do a man's job.

It all makes me feel like we're excusing ourselves for being women. We want to do this job but think it belongs to a man, so we feel like we should dress the part. I took the risk on my most recent draft of a resume to call myself an artist and a scientist. It's a risk because, generally, search committees think they're looking for an administrator. And they're looking for a man. Why would any of us think it better to imitate a man than to be a genuine woman, if a woman is what you are?

I've never entertained so much conversation, or rather, I should say comments, about the shoes I wear than in my last parish. Not only is the pulpit open brass-work at St. Anne's, and includes an optional platform for short people, which I prefer to call my perch, but the pews come up to within three feet of the pulpit, so for about the first six pews no one sees anything except my feet. Just my feet with my voice. How can they not notice my shoes, and pay attention to my feet?

So, I've taken a bit of license. Though I don't preach barefoot, I've worn my combat boots in Advent, I've preached about my dad's organ shoes and the slippers my daughter Caroline gave me for my birthday, and I've dangled my running shoes as a reminder to join me on the diocesan hunger walk. Feet. Bare feet. Boots and shoes.

I've kept the custom of wearing closed-toed shoes in all my parish settings because people kneel at the communion rail, which puts them within range of careful visuals of my toes. Not something I think people should have to be conscious of when feasting on the body and blood of Christ.

One Sunday at St. Thomas my heels with the crate made me too tall, but without the crate I was too short. So, I popped them off and used the crate barefoot. I found it energizing, and secretive, and a little on the spectacular side. It gave me the ability to move, and stand on tiptoe, and for some reason made me feel like a real preacher. I didn't jump, or dance a jig, but sometimes I felt like it. There's a good precedent for bare feet. It's protocol for holy ground and acknowledging that we are in God's presence.

The very notion of holy ground, that ground can be filled with God, is enticing and promises me the possibility of tripping into something utterly beyond myself, and all-consuming, at any given moment. Moses heard God's voice from the fire. Transcendence and immanence. An early discovery that the Holy One manifests in the material substance of our physical existence. God as Holy and Other, above and beyond our existence, shows up in ordinary stuff. God's presence in the earth, underfoot, in the fire in a shrubbery, all invitation to expect God in the next breath or sideways glance.

The voices we hear, the uncanny sense of the Divine, the certainty that God is in the elements of earth and fire, suddenly make us feel we should do something about our feet. Moses took off his shoes. Great idea.

Initiative for Prayer

Prayer as Listening to Your Feet

Our feet have been with us all our days. Consider how knowing they are. And how they accompany us and carry us, without ever much being appreciated or acknowledged. Feet provide another way of knowing for us. Bare feet on holy ground know God.

Have a seat, and take off your shoes, or whatever footwear you might have on your feet.

Just have a long look at them. How are they alike or different? How do they show the years of trodding for you? Think a little about where you and your feet have been over the years.

Ask your feet what they know. Ask them what they can tell you about holy ground. Ask them to tell you when they knew you were in the animated presence of God, either in the earth or in a burning bush, but you didn't notice. Jot down a few things in your journal, or perhaps a prayer of thanksgiving for your feet.

> The Lord appeared to him in a flame of fire out of a bush. . . . God called to him out of the bush, "Moses, Moses!" And he said, "Here I am." (Exodus 3:2, 4)

A bush that burns but is not consumed; from it a voice, and around it, bare feet for holy ground. Flame, tongues of fire. God. A God who wants to be known. A God who takes on form, and voice, and fiery flame. A story that is appointed some years during the season of Epiphany. A season of knowing, and seeing, and revelation. The season when God is revealed and known in such things as fire, and water, and bread, and wine, and human flesh. All material substance that manifests God.

A God who wants to be known. A God who says God's own name, and yours. A God who touches down. But some years we read about Moses, and the bush that burns, deep in the season of Pentecost, and so then it is a different thing for us. The Day of Pentecost is a day. One single day, a festival day in the church, when we wear red, drape our furniture with the color of fire, and fly kites. A single day, for play acting, when God comes in, and lights in tongues of fire on his people, and fills them with Holy Spirit. A God who would be known, and named, a self-revealing God, for our seeing.

But the season of Pentecost is not a festival day. It is a long ordinary season, and for that we change the color to green, for life, and growth, and going out into the world. And for weeks and weeks, from somewhere in mid-May or early June, all the way until Advent in December, we wear green. Green for the season of Pentecost, and what we call Ordinary Time. The Ordinary Time in which we live, the regular stuff—not much pageantry, ordinary things like most of life.

The ordinary living part. The mundane, the routine, the ritual of things like brushing teeth, and washing dishes, and finishing homework, and driving a car all around town, and charging the batteries in the cell phone, and paying bills, and cooking, and eating. The regular, routine, Ordinary Time, where we find ourselves between feast days, which is most of the days in a life. Ordinary life. It's not Christmas. It's not Easter. It's not All Saints' Day. It's in-between.

Some years, the lectionary places the Exodus text with Moses stopping at this bush that burns but is not consumed, and taking off his shoes to have a conversation of magnanimous proportion with God, is read in Ordinary Time. Fed to us like daily fare for a long season of living—the in-between time—as though we might expect such things to happen on a regular basis, in a regular sort of way. To suggest, perhaps, that it is for the ordinary life and regular folk, that this God would choose to say our names and want to be known. A love life of the most ordinary sort: a daily fare of God incarnate, a regular and routine life with God. Not unlike the end of day's rest when you put down your head, or the phone call to remind you to pick up milk and bread. An ordinary love life not unlike conversation and tears, or argument, or waking up to a loved one, to coffee and breakfast, or singing and dancing on the porch in wind and rain. God in the material substance, and the ordinary ways of knowing. The way you and I know each other. And the way we live our lives, in the body. This God, who says his name.

Moses says in essence, "Well, for practical purposes, I need to be able to tell them who sent me. So, what is your name? Who should I tell them, sent me?" And God says, "The God of Abraham, the God of Isaac, and the God of Jacob" (Exodus 3:6). There, tell them that.

I guess it's not what you know but who you know. Because everybody knows, Moses knows, you and I know, who Abraham, Isaac, and Jacob are, in the Genesis saga. They are the patriarchs. And we know all their wild and extraordinary tales of rather ordinary lives. They are all too familiar. They are so ordinary that we could write their sagas from the pages of our own journals. But that is how God says he should be known. By the life he lives with his people. Tell them who sent you, Moses, "The God of Abraham, the God of Isaac, and the God of Jacob." The three of these. All of them. And that is who God claims to be. God is the God who says, "I'm with them." The transcendent God, immanent. Present. The God of Abraham, Isaac, and Jacob. Tell them that, Moses.

For nearly a year, little four-year-old Ruthie Wade had practiced the spirituality of transcendence. Ruthie had established a relationship with her little sister, Ginny. Ginny, for whom we gave thanks in every Eucharistic prayer in the course of a year, when we name the names of those among us who have died.

Vigilant, as she took leave and let go of her baby sister, Ruthie learned to keep the conversation daily, with and about her infant sister. The kind of conversation that keeps and treasures and fans the flame of a life, a real but transcendent life, to make it present and with us, now. A knowing that is beyond knowing, beyond the limits of the ordinary and material experience.

A tall order for any of us, but surely beyond the capacity of a four-year-old. A high-end spirituality. Sophisticated, and delicate, and sensitive to exquisite subtlety. Ruthie already knows more than most of us ever will about transcendence. And how to hover in the midst and maintain the delicate tension between presence and absence; holy and profane; knowing the unknowable; and tending the soul capacity; and how to converse with wisdom in the grocery store about her unseen sister; and bearing witness to a family of four when only three sit at the dinner table. She knows the sameness of visible and invisible. "Immortal, invisible, God only wise, in light inaccessible hid from our eyes."[45]

For nearly a year, Ruthie did the spiritual work. She learned the language of grief, and talked, and prayed, and drew pictures of it. She practiced the spirituality of waiting, for this new baby, "Martha," to be born. And in her own tiny little self she occupied the place of that tenuous clinging to hope, and promise; even when hope, and promise had been dashed before.

Ruthie has plowed the tough ground of the valley of dry bones and has come up answering the question God asked of Ezekiel; the one Ezekiel pitched back to God when God asked, "Can these bones live?" (Ezekiel 37:3). Ezekiel skirted, but Ruthie answered, "Yes, Lord, these bones can live." And they do because she knows her little sister lives with God. Ginny is in heaven. And Ruthie will tell you so. She will tell you about a transcendent spirituality that is imminent.

Ruthie already knows God. She keeps company with the patriarchs who bear witness to God's name for Moses. She knows what they know, the three of them, our Abraham, Isaac, and Jacob, that God is present in the material substance of this life, and all creation.

Look at the stars, Abram. Gaze up at heaven's night sky and see if you can count the stars (Genesis 15:5). God's promise for descendants, the generations yet unborn. Look up and believe me for it, Abram. Ruthie believes it and is counting the stars in expectation.

And Sarah's Son of Laughter, Isaac, with his father, clamoring about on a mountainside. You, Isaac, are the sacrifice that lives, stay alive and live it out for me (Genesis 22:5–14). Ruthie is such a sacrifice; she is the one that lives, after a brush with death such that you feel the slip of the blade on your own neck.

And Jacob, who laid it down at heaven's gate one night, and slept, and the angels of God came and went. Angels, up and down the ladder, and God too. Take your rest here, Jacob, at this thin place where heaven and earth are joined, and I will stand beside you while you sleep (Genesis 28:11–17). Ruthie has slept there at just such a gate, where the company of heaven comes, and goes, and tends you in your rest and weariness.

The patriarchs bear witness to God's name for Moses. Tell them that's who I am, Moses. The God of Abraham, Isaac, and Jacob. Ruthie could tell Moses all about this God. Names. People. Story of the sacred in the mundane. Earth, and sky, and stars, and holy ground, and the hosts of heaven who walk the earth, and the blood of a sacrifice that lives. And there, for Moses, this God of Abraham, Isaac, and Jacob manifests in fire and flame and hallows the ground.

After a year of practicing her transcendent spirituality, and keeping company with patriarchs and prophets, Ruthie keeps company this weekend with the likes of Moses. She is at the burning bush, in fact she dances around barefoot on tiptoes, and buck naked on holy ground. She did her barefoot dance in the bathtub when she got the news about baby Martha.

Moses debated with God, about God's credibility. His exact identity. Authority. He wanted plans, and maps, and instructions. Ruthie just said what Moses was trying to say, "Martha is here on earth! Can you believe it?" Full-body Celtic celebration of God incarnate. God from heaven in earth made known. God made known in human form. Ruthie gets it. Transcendent and immanent.

"God is here on earth. . . . Can you believe it?"

Don't you think that's what Moses wanted to say? God is not just up there, where the rest of us might like God to stay. God in fire for the long season of Pentecost, like it is just the most ordinary, everyday thing, that we might expect to stumble across the presence of God in fire. Moses stops for fire at this bush. Moses leans in close for fire at this bush that burns but is not consumed, and from it a voice. Moses takes off his shoes for fire at this bush, bare feet, on holy ground. To suggest, perhaps, that it is for the ordinary life, and regular folk like you and me, that this God would choose to say his name, and want to be known. His invitation in form, and voice, and fiery flame, to a love life of the most ordinary kind, and the daily fare of God incarnate. An everyday, holy life, of grocery store tales, of how it is just the most ordinary nonchalant thing, that God, and all the company of heaven, are coming and going all in and around this holy ground. And that we should all be barefoot. Because as Ruthie would say, for Moses: "God is here on earth. . . . Can you believe it?!"

Initiative for Prayer

Prayer as Bare Feet

Bare feet and God on holy ground.

Choose this prayer initiative only to the extent that you can do this practice in a safe way. Find a cemetery that you're comfortable with. Take your journal and a thick votive or pillar candle, with matches. It doesn't have to be completely dark for this initiative. Give yourself some time to settle into the space. Take a little walk with your lighted candle, and look at some of the names, and dates, on the head stones.

Take off your shoes. Stand and feel the earth under your feet. Walk around the cemetery, and name the names on the stones, and call them out. Place your candle on the ground. Imagine the nature of the transcendent God, imminent. Ask the patriarchs what they might have to say to you about the presence of God. Imagine yourself at heaven's gate. Lie down. Ask God to tend your rest and keep you. Name some names of your own matriarchs, and patriarchs, who have gone ahead of you, and ask them how to live in the full presence of God. Write some thoughts in your journal.

God in Water

*To include mist, fog, steam, rain,
sea, river, stream, creek, wave,
puddle, fountain, and spring.*

The smell of gold bar Dial soap can bring back a summer's night after a long day of play. Lying in the bed with the windows open and seersucker pajamas after a bath. The pleasure of exhaustion and the promise of renewal.

My grandfather used to make soap. In the big claw foot tub, he would mix lye and other dangerous ingredients that miraculously came out in pleasing rough chunks, cube-shaped and slippery, that could do magic. Stains out of everything, from linens, and laundry, and the bottom of your feet. Lipstick and boot black both. Homemade soap that did wonders, even for the human soul. Sometimes I buy it at the French market, just to remember.

My grandmother used to soak. As one who wore sensible shoes and exercised the flair of practical wisdom, she took that kind of time for herself, and bathed so hot that she came out wrinkled, and pink, and still a little moist, pleased with herself, like she'd been reborn. In fact, she stayed so long, I would conduct a secret quiz, asking her questions that only she would know the answers to in case she had become someone else during the soak. Bathing can do that, and I knew it.

A holy bath and ritual washing. We pour, splash, sprinkle, and scrub our way into the kingdom of God. Ablutions. A font of marble, granite, or hollowed stone for a basin, round like the womb and full of water. We wash. We begin again. We are reborn. The lavabo, a lavabo bowl, a lavabo towel, and an acolyte for pouring water over the celebrant's hands for purification, and consecration. Because God is in the element of water. We know what ritual, and liturgy, are about, because water is common, and ordinary, and very everyday, and full of God. We tend the flesh. Citrus and eucalyptus, oil of olives, and salt from the sea. The physical is spiritual, the spiritual is physical, and God is in the water.

God is in the element of water for bathing. For getting clean. Fresh. Scrubbed. Spotless. Organic extracts. Both sweet and pungent. Washing away sin, and sorrow. Lye and other such dangerous cleansing ingredients that suit us for regrets—so much so that we add a luffa sea sponge for our need to exfoliate.

God is in the element of water for getting well. The long soak and immersing ourselves for restoration and relaxation. And then there are the fever baths, or the cool washcloth on the forehead, and pressed against cheeks. Naaman with his leprosy dipping no less than seven times in the Jordan's muddy waters, and out he came with skin like a young boy's. Healed. All new (2 Kings 5:14). Not unlike my grand-mother.

God is in the element of water for being born. The font of our being, and the source of life. The prenatal swim of fetus, and the deep, out of which God called all things into being.

God is in the element of water for being rescued. The Lord makes "a way in the sea, a path in the mighty waters" (Isaiah 43:16) for an exodus. Water, the source of our liberation from bondage. An angel carried a jar of water for Elijah, not once, but twice, to save his life when he laid down to die in the wilderness (1 Kings 19:4–6). Water, the source of our salvation.

God is in the element of water for consecration. Being set apart for God, and the spa-like Levitical practice of ordination for priesthood. Moses washed Aaron and his sons with water. Then he put tunic, and tied a sash, and wrapped with robe, and ephod, and a special woven waistband, then a turban on his head with a gold plate, and sacred diadem. Then, he poured some of the oil on Aaron's head and anointed him to consecrate him. Setting him apart for God. The kind of ritual we understand because we do it every day. We get ready, and we use water to do it. Our consecra-tion. Our ordination. Yours and mine.

God is in the element of water for our everyday God-love. Our every-day grooming, primping, preening, spa moments; these are our practice of baptism, our daily consecration. Loofah, and lava, gold, and gem adorn-ing, head wrap, and fragrant oil pouring. Our everyday dedication of this body to God. To love God with our bodies.

God is in the element of water. Water for our holy life, to immerse ourselves, to drink, and gulp ourselves full, to splash and play our way to unfathomable satisfaction, and want, of God.

The element of water is the substance of Incarnation, because it is the way humans are born. It is the means for becoming human. God in the humanity of earthenware jars, and the uncontainable Holy One of living water. God in the humanity of a young woman's womb, and the uncon-trollable holy water of birthing. God in the humanity of John, with rites of baptism, and the unchecked possibility of the holy Incarnate One, getting in the water with him.

God is in the element of water, but even more than that, all that has come into being is born of that God-water. The element of water is a theophany. In *The Book of Creation*, J. Philip Newell writes of Eriugena interpreting the waters of Genesis chapter 1

> as the dark mystery of God that enfolds all things. Into this essentially unknowable and infinite realm of God a dome of space and time is created. It is like a womb or matrix of life. In it will appear all that is to be created. . . . All that is born in this matrix of life has its conception in the Infinite. Creation's life partakes of the essence of God's life, and to that extent is a theophany or manifestation of the mystery of God.[46]

All of the elements, earth, air, fire, and water, can be understood as "in a whirlwind of motion," as the wind of God "sweeps over the face of the waters" on the first day of creation, and on the second day, "can be viewed as the ongoing explosion of elemental particles hurtling through space."[47] God's own being, the matter and substance of all that is.

On the third night of moon rises, I watched and waited from my screened porch, but the moon never rose over the treetops at the water's edge on Long Island Sound, where it had been the night before, when it rose up in perfect fullness right in front of me. So, I roused myself from the rocking chair to investigate, and there, far to the northern end of the shore, I saw a slightly waning moon, so heavy with sacred fire that it labored long to lift above the horizon, round and red-orange as the interior flesh of a tree-ripened peach. Oh my. To worship the Beauty of Holiness.

This Mercy by the Sea Retreat and Conference Center, a perfect place for being schooled in Celtic consciousness with J. Philip Newell because Celtic consciousness is a matter of being aware that all creation is sacred, and letting that awareness change your life. It is keeping a spiritual practice of paying attention to the presence of God in all things, and listening. Sea breeze and bird wing; earth in sand, and shell, stacked stone, and round rock; salt water lapping a lullaby, and rain in deluge; fire by day, moon by night, all for our listening for the heartbeat of God, because God is an elemental God.

Mercy by the Sea is a *finis terra* kind of place, where land meets sea, and it seems you are at the end of the earth where God says, to you, as to Isaiah, "Listen . . . O coastlands" (Isaiah 49:1).

9

OVER IT, THROUGH IT, IN IT

The irony of a formula when applied to religion is that it produces the opposite of the intended effect. Or at least it can and has for me. Formulas are about predictable outcome, certainties, guarantees. Proof. All the things people want religion to deliver. All in a recipe.

When we were growing up, we were taught what was called the sinner's prayer. A formula. It was the way of salvation and contained all the component parts of being born again. A combination that would open the gates of heaven to the likes of me, or anyone else who said all the words, and with just the right sincerity of heart. That's where a formula breaks down—when the human factor is the variable.

When the human factor was me, the religious formulaic prayer did nothing but make me insecure. Less sure. Unsure. Doubtful that I did it in just such a way that the afterlife was locked in for me. Heaven, the desired outcome, as opposed to hell.

It takes a whole life lived and died to find out for sure, and I always worried. Maybe I left out one of the component parts, some critical, fatal detail. And I wouldn't know it until I stood at the pearly gates and they did not, in fact, open. High stakes. Or maybe I didn't have the right measure of faith, or maybe my sincerity was a little too watery, but who could know such matters of the heart?

But it was a simple prayer of salvation. Who couldn't do that and enjoy a lifetime of peace? In fact, you could use the prayer to convert others. We were trained to lead another person through their conversion by telling them to repeat the phrases of the prayer after us, one at a time, and they too would be saved. All the necessary parts were included in the prayer. It was meant to help you know you were saved. It made me almost certain that I wasn't.

It didn't make sense that something like the salvation experience could be so universally identical. The sameness of it. Everyone, everywhere. The manipulation of God, and the kingdom of God, with a turnkey formula? Would that really work?

Baptism was the same sort of gadget. Believer's baptism was to be performed only after a person was saved and had said the sinner's prayer. Immersion into a pool of water, whether a tank in a church, a fountain if it was huge like something in a town square, or it could be an open lake, or stream, or river, but it had to be big enough to get into, and not a font with a bowl for cupping the water, and no sprinkling. That would be infant baptism, and how could an infant be saved? They can't even say the sinner's prayer, much less mean it.

In my early days as an Episcopalian, I was still a little nervous about that certainty thing. And what were we doing, baptizing babies? Did we risk taking away their chance to really secure their salvation? Were we giving them false confidence and thereby derailing the way of salvation for them? Always I reminded myself, the formula doesn't work anyway, and I know it.

I have found my place, my comfort, my peace, in a different ritual: the ritual of sacrament. Perhaps it is exchanging one formula for another. But if it is, then at least with this particular formula the variable isn't me. It's the water. Celtic sensibilities shift me from formula, and proper maneuvering, to a simple recognition of God in all of creation, and most especially in this case, in the water. The water of baptism is holy water because God is in it. No hocus-pocus. I don't have to do or manipulate anything. God is, present. And I can rest in it. In fact, I can celebrate it.

The language about the water in sacrament is not scientific formula, but it is the language of poetry, the metaphor of sacrament, and the custom of storytelling. The water tells stories. About God. About the people of God. About us. About me. The factor isn't the human factor, it is the divine factor. The action is God's action, not mine. The creating, the saving, the hallowing, God does all of it in the water, because God is in the water. So, I can find God there. My salvation becomes existential, and my knowing God becomes simply a matter of being immersed in God, and seeing the divine in the face of the other, or even in my own face, or in the world about me. And in the water.

When we perform sacraments, like the sacrament of baptism, we use the water to tell the story about what God has done, is doing. We tell a truth, declare it, pronounce it, and celebrate it. We don't actually make something happen, so I still can't muck it up by getting it wrong.

Initiative for Prayer

Prayer as Concocting a Formula

Scout around on the internet for a formula, a recipe for a salt scrub or sugar scrub. Choose a simple one for which you might already have the ingredients around the house.

Collect the ingredients and follow the recipe. Did you choose something fresh with citrus, or earthy like clove? As you add each ingredient, ponder the presence of God in it, with a prayer of thanksgiving.

Use your scrub as a prayer practice, reflecting on the organic nature of your product. Consider your relationship with God, and the organic nature of a life with God.

How is the luxuriating use of the scrub different from the list of ingredients and the directions? How is a relationship different from a formula? Write some thoughts in your journal about this act of body love. Ask the scrub what it has to say to you about being in relationship with the Divine, and write about it.

> I looked, and there was a great multitude that no one could count, from every nation, from all tribes and peoples and languages, standing before the throne and before the Lamb, robed in white, with palm branches in their hands. (Revelation 7:9)

With the full capacity of memory, and no-holds-barred celebration, we summon all saints, all martyrs, and all the faithful departed of all souls. The Celts keep company with the saints and talk to them as though they're right there at the table with them or accompanying them in their daily chores. Celtic spirituality would have us live this way, every day. But for the church, All Saints' Day is a peculiar day that recollects every trip we have ever made to the grave, and echoes with the song we sing there, as we sing it again and still and always: Alleluia, Alleluia, Alleluia.

All Saints' Day positions us resolutely in the Communion of Saints: a patron saint of hat makers. The first of March for David of Wales and, too, his cousins Patrick and Brigit. Saint Swithens in the Swamp, and Nicholas of Myra protecting children from being sold into slavery. All of them, with all of us, on parade and in procession, with decorated crosses on long sticks. We name names and keep company with the beloved departed. This strange day, this All Saints'. This high feast day of celebration, and commemoration, and conjuring the dead.

We pull out all the stops of spiritual symbol and gesture. We gather around the font in white garments and liturgical garb. Flame from the great Paschal candle leaps out in small torches for children. Oil of chrism for crosses on foreheads. And then of course, there is: The Water. And God over it, and through it, and in it. Over it in creation. Through it, in redemption. In it, in incarnation.

All of salvation history, in a day. All of a piece, in one bowl of water, a one-act drama with God as the singular actor: God creates. God redeems. God becomes human. In one fell swoop, for all these babies to be baptized, for the dead in Christ, for all the saints, and for you and me who count ourselves among them, God is in the water, and God acts. In one sacred bowl of water, we are brought into being in creation, liberated from bondage in the Exodus, made holy in our humanity with the company of Jesus.

Initiative for Prayer

Prayer as Roll Call and Splashing

Fill a bowl with water. The bowl should be small enough to carry in one arm but large enough to be generous with water. Cut a sprig of rosemary or pine bough. Go outside. Walk around your house or neighborhood performing the asperges. This is the rite of sprinkling a congregation with holy water. While you walk, dip your branch into the water and fling the water with a celebratory flair. As you go, call out names who have been saints in your life. People who have been the presence of God for you. When you pause to think, just call out the song we sing at the grave: Alleluia, Alleluia, Alleluia.

On another day, you might visit a cemetery and try this, calling out the names on grave markers, and blessing them with your holy water.

If we like to experiment with high church liturgy, we can be more playful with our ritual, and the clergy come round with a bowl of water, and a sprig of rosemary, and spritz and splash the whole lot of the congregation. If we're a bit of a more broad-minded church, we can be more dramatic about it and dunk you down into a pool of water up over your heads. But as it is, as it always is, there is the gift of water for the celebration of baptism. And God is over it, through it, and in it. We tell stories around the font, and the water in the bowl becomes something different than it is, because of the stories. Something big. Something untamable, undoable.

"Over it," we say in the story, "the Holy Spirit moved in the beginning of creation."[48] And with that, the water becomes the abyss, the deep darkness, the chaos. The chance for a do-over. On any given day, I may need to start again. Maybe just a moment in the day itself. Maybe an experience in my memory, or relationship, or maybe, just my whole life, and needing to start over.

And with a touch of water, a splash of holy water from the font, I can invite, beg, plead, implore, the wind of God to sweep over me, to stretch out over the abyss that is me. Me, the deep darkness; me, the chaos. Me, the great deep. And make me born again. Bring me into being, again. Start over. Speak my name and wake me up. Refresh, renew, recreate. Make something of me. Something new, and infant, and innocent. A life worth swaddling, treasuring, nurturing to fruition, or at least until lunchtime, before I need all over again, to start all over again. Every baptism a nativity. Every splash of holy water my birthing.

Initiative for Prayer

Prayer as Reflective Intercession

The water in the font at baptism becomes something different because we pray the stories of creation, redemption, and incarnation over the water. We recall the stories of what God has done, the stories of God's saving acts, with the words, over it, through it, in it.

Challenge yourself to focus on the stories, on God, and the acts of God in the water, and the gifts of baptism that are available to us.

Make a list of some of your loved ones. Pray their baptism. With the thought of each person on your list, consider which of these three stories they might need most today, and bless them in your prayers with that holy water. Your own reflections and intercessions will go further, broader, and deeper than this, but here's a place to start, here are some ways to pray the water of baptism for any given person on your list, in three parts:

The Water of Creation

Part One

Does he seem to need to begin again, a fresh start, even if it's only nine o'clock in the morning and he just headed out the door? Does she need to know deep down that she is God's good creation, and that she pleases God? Pray God's brooding, hovering spirit over the deep waters of someone's soul, that God will bring forth life. Pray that God will speak his name, and that he will come into being, or that she will hear God saying hers, and get up.

"Through it," we say in the story, "you led the children of Israel out of their bondage in Egypt into the land of promise,"[49] and the water becomes the Red Sea, our breaking loose. Our escape. Our running from slavery, our jumping off, and out. Our breaking free. Our running through deep water on dry ground. Footing on solid ground. And with a scallop shell full, I pour it on my head, trickling down my back, and swirling into the cup of my collar bone.

God is in the water, championing me to run like the wind. The sweat from my pores, the salt crusting at my ears and along my jawbone. In holy water I can conjure passion and muster courage. I can gather gumption and gusto. I can run. Run from captors, flee from bondage, escape slavery. Break free. With the holy water from the font I can be off and running with muscle, and sinew, and pounding heart, I can break out from the bonds of slavery. Chariots racing in the background intent on doing battle with me, hammering at my heels to crush; horses' hooves beating the ground, their eyes wide. Headlong into holy water that breaks open like walls flanking to left and to right, held at bay, for my passage. To be free. Born to myself. Owned by no one anymore. Ever.

Initiative for Prayer

Prayer as Reflective Intercession

The Water of Redemption

Part Two

Who in your household, or on the prayer list you made of loved ones, is lifting backbreaking burdens of servitude, oppression, or hard labor of any sort?

Pray God to lead them through to liberation.

Is someone trying to break a habit, change their ways, or listen to their own voice instead of the demands of someone else? Is someone bound to a life they can't live, and in need of a Moses to lead them out? Pray for God to part the waters for them.

Pray for someone who is far from home and needs a way through deep water.

"In it," we say in the story, "your Son Jesus received the baptism of John and was anointed by the Holy Spirit,"[50] and with that, the water becomes the Garden of Eden. The hallowing of humanity. God in the humanity of John with his rites of baptism in the Jordan River and the unchecked possibility of Jesus getting in the water with him. God in the flesh, born of water, human. A second Adam. There, with his cousin John, his human family, and their common DNA from birth mothers. Jesus and John comingling. This Jordan River birth water. Face to face and bathing for holiness.

Who could dare to bathe with God? But Jesus says, "I'm coming in." And John says, "Ah, but . . . no"—and then, "Yes," to the holy water and God in it. The holy hallowed flesh of Jesus, and John, and now all of humanity. Comingled. Our innocence restored to innocence. Naked and glistening. Flesh revealed. No garments sewn for hiding, no covering up. And with a foot in or an elbow, with a bowl full of holy water or my full immersion in the Jordan River, God calls me out of hiding. "Who told you that you were naked?" (Genesis 3:11), and baptism becomes our unknowing.

Unknowing our shame. Unknowing our unworthiness. Unknowing our rejected, broken, deficient selves. Unknowing sin. And separation. Face to face, nose to nose, eye to eye, naked before God, and unashamed. This is the unchecked possibility of Jesus getting in the water with us: we will be seen. Out of hiding, and all of humanity, out of hiding. Now, no more condemnation.

Babies at baptism give us our posture: reclined in the love of God. Lifted. Borne up. Swaddled. Scooped. Enveloped in the love of God.

All of salvation history in one act, begun and completed. Whether we go kicking and screaming, or sleep our way through it, we exist in the love of God, from our creation to our redemption, to the holy incarnate life we live, all of a moment, cradled in the heart of God. Like the babies, we will sleep, or laugh, or protest the water, which for all we're worth is the vast love of God.

The font at baptism is our storytelling bowl. Water brings me God. The water can tell and retell my story. The water can make me live again. A new story.

Initiative for Prayer

Prayer as Reflective Intercession

Water of Incarnation

Part Three

For each person on your prayer list, pray for them to know deep down that their humanity is holy, their body hallowed. Pray that each person can see the face of Christ when they look in the mirror. Which one needs to know they are the image and likeness of God, and that Jesus looks like us? Pray that one or another on your list will delight in the bodily beauty of being human.

Pray that each person can enter the water of incarnation and be a new Adam, a new Eve. That each one will individually come out of hiding, and know they are seen, and loved, and welcomed, by God.

While I'm kind of thankful for the artists' rendering of a loincloth for the crucified Jesus, history suggests that the crucified were naked. Strip a person bare and show their nakedness. Shaming behavior. And brutal exposure. Jesus, pure, and holy, suffered our shame, not as in the atonement and the cosmic swap, but as in his being human. As in his being stripped bare and naked.

Shame alludes to our Genesis story. The water of baptism mirrors our Eden image. We look into the font, and see the glory of creation, and man, and woman, in it, as the story says: "both naked" and "not ashamed" (Genesis 2:25). Getting in the water of baptism means we strip down. We are naked and not ashamed. Not hiding in the shrubbery. Not slowly sewing fig leaves. And meeting God in the garden in the cool of the day, for an evening stroll.

That's the water we dip into, water that is full of God and shamelessness. We immerse ourselves in that reality and take it on as our truth. Humanity, nakedness, knowing, honoring. Seeing and being seen. And not ashamed. Water is the stuff of which we are made. It is in our human being to be made mostly of water. It is the ubiquitous substance of human life. For a Celtic shepherd on a hillside, God is in the water of the rain, and the wave of the sea, and in the well for our drawing out. God, immediate, and present in the elements. Water universally necessary, and immediately accessible, and the common unifying element of our humanity. Water for a sacramental act enfolds all of humanity into the return to Eden, and the shedding of shame.

But there's this sticky Bible verse not only in Mark 8, but also in Luke 9, where Jesus says that if we are ashamed of him when he comes in glory, then he will be ashamed of us.

It's startling, upsetting, horrifying even, that he would say such a thing out loud and articulate my worst nightmare. It picks at my anxiety that I got the childhood formula wrong and will be, in the end, excluded from the kingdom come. How could we be stuck in a bramble of shame with the Son of God; no wait, the gospels say, Mark and Luke say, the Son of Man. Jesus self-identified with us by the title used to emphasize his humanity. His commonality. He is the Son of Man. He is every man and every woman, so to speak. He is born of water, and emerges from the womb, like all the rest of us. A universal identity.

Lent begins the liturgy with the penitential order, and the circumnavigation of the nave. Lent begins with the Great Litany, and triggers an avalanche of every possible scenario by which we can sin: "all blindness of heart; from pride, vainglory and hypocrisy; from envy, hatred, malice; . . . from all inordinate and sinful affections; and from all the deceits of the world, the flesh and the devil; oppression, conspiracy, and rebellion; from violence, battle, and murder. . . ."[51]

We all know it's all true for all of us. That's why we say it, I guess. To acknowledge it. Admit it. Ideally, it means we can be done with it. That it is finished. And yet, what about this hiding thing we do?

Celtic wisdom is effusive about all of creation being permeated with God. For me, that reaches far enough to mean that our shared humanity with Christ is, actually and literally, shared, in our birth water, as is his glory. Is it too much to behold and embrace the full humanity and complete divinity of Christ, and to think we share all of that with him? And that the same is true of all creation, which is utterly physical, and material, and yet at the same time, completely sacred. We are tangled up in the brambles, with the Son of Man.

Our humanity is so entwined with his that if we are ashamed of our humanity, then he is ashamed of his, which is ours. We lock it down between the two of us, into shame. We are so one with the Incarnate Christ that shame covers both of us, or neither of us. If we are ashamed of ourselves, it is the same as being ashamed of him. We are so much one and the same that the shame of our own human being extends to him, and makes him ashamed, too. He is in it with us. In the shame, and the dread scenario of Mark 8 and Luke 9. I admit that it's a totally awkward thing to imagine Jesus naked, but in as much as we cover Jesus up in our artwork, we cover up ourselves in real life.

Loincloths notwithstanding, to look away from the naked cruciform is to engage in shaming behavior. We think its kind and polite, and has something to do with personal privacy, but ultimately it suggests that he should not be seen. He should be hidden from view. We imagine that he would be embarrassed if we looked on, and embarrassment is the flush of shame.

The work of Lent is to look. To look at him, not in order to shame him, but to behold his fully human, fully sacred body, with honor, awe, and majesty. The work of Lent is to not cover ourselves with layer upon layer upon layer of fig leaves, burying ourselves in the decaying matter of our mortality, but to look. To see our own holy bodies, with the same honor, awe, and majesty. I can only imagine that this is why baptism became a sacrament, because immersing ourselves in the same holy water, and swimming around with God, can change our experience of what it means to be truly human. The element of water can transform us. The element of water can cleanse, shed, rebirth. The element of water can restore our joy, and delight, in our Eden identity.

What would it take for me to live in glory? Right here, and right now, in the Eden life afforded me in the holy birth water of baptism. What would it take for me to let go of shame, all shaming moments, all shame experiences in my life, that shrink my soul with darkness, and hiding, and to live in glory?

Just an interesting side note: history also suggests that the candidates for Holy Baptism in the early years of the church were naked.

Initiative for Prayer

Prayer as Affirming the Image of Christ

Purchase an inexpensive full-length mirror. Attach seashells to the frame of the mirror. Let these symbolize the water of creation and incarnation, and the water of which you were born. These can be inexpensive manmade shells purchased at a craft store and hot glued to the frame. Or you can forgo the permanent quality of gluing shells, and simply print out web-based photos of shells. Cut them out and affix them to the frame of the new mirror, or one you already have.

Consider your image in front of the mirror. Stand naked and look at yourself. Speak of love and adoration. Talk to yourself about shame. About image. About hiding. About holiness. Speak to the Christ in you.

Consider your image reflected back to you, as the image of Christ. Try some prayers as you gaze at your hallowed humanity. Here are some examples if it helps you get going:

Try the language of the anthems for Good Friday.

"We adore you, O Christ, and we bless you,
because by your holy cross you have redeemed the world."[52]

Here are some words from the Genesis story:

Then God said, "Let us make humankind in our image, according to our likeness;" ... So, God created humankind in his image, in the image of God he created them; male and female he created them.... God saw everything that he had made, and indeed, it was very good. And there was evening and there was morning, the sixth day. (Genesis 1:26–31)

Or, create a personal rendition of this affirmation of our physical being:

They were "naked, and were not ashamed" (Genesis 2:25).

Read Proverbs 8:27–31, where Wisdom frolics in the creation of the world:

When he established the heavens, I was there,
when he drew a circle on the face of the deep,

when he made firm the skies above,
when he established the fountains of the deep,

when he assigned to the sea its limit,

so that the waters might not transgress his command,

when he marked out the foundations of the earth,

then I was beside him, like a master worker;

and I was daily his delight,

rejoicing before him always,

rejoicing in his inhabited world

and delighting in the human race.

Memorize and recite Psalm 139:13–16:

For it was you who formed my inward parts;
you knit me together in my mother's womb.
I praise you, for I am fearfully and wonderfully made.
Wonderful are your works;
that I know very well.
My frame was not hidden from you,
when I was being made in secret,
intricately woven in the depths of the earth.
Your eyes beheld my unformed substance.
In your book were written
all the days that were formed for me,
when none of them as yet existed.

If poetry isn't as appealing to you, try the legal language of Paul in the Letter to the Romans: "There is therefore now no condemnation for those who are in Christ Jesus. For the law of the Spirit of life in Christ Jesus has set you free from the law of sin and death" (Romans 8:1–2).

———

10

IT IS FINISHED

We took up the towel and washed feet last night. It was Maundy Thursday, which is when we imitate Jesus's washing his disciples' feet, as an act of love and service. We filled clay basins with warm water, and stacked towels for a ritual, and used feet for a symbol that intensifies our commonality. Our feet. We washed each other's feet.

Dancing feet, feet that twirl, feet that dash, and kick, and leap, and bound for a jump shot. Feet still trailing dust particles from France. Feet just in from California. Feet wrapped in pink suede. Some on fashionable platforms for scaling better heights. Eighty-year-old feet that trek the Camp Mikell Cross Hike like hinds' feet on high places. Feet bogged down in slow steps of thick sorrow. Feet that walk the halls of justice. Feet that fight for freedom and peace. Feet that fly far to do mercy in the lands Africa and Asia. Feet that need wheels, and a chair that folds up. Crumpled feet. Crooked feet. Feet worn thin, and roughed up thick with callus. Feet that stand up, stand with, and stand for. Yellow rain boots on her way out the door, just this morning. We walk.

The sea of humanity. The throngs. Our common ground there in our feet; and under our feet, the ground. Earth. Humus. Human. Our common humanity. Feet that stand still and stay. A mother's feet stopped from her busyness. To stand. There. At the foot of the cross.

Stained glass. Lead veins in a sacristy window with three crosses on a hill, three figures in purple glass, nailed to the wood, the middle with a tri-radial nimbus, the way of an artist to render the Holy One. In the foreground, three women looking on. God on a cross. God in human form. Jesus at the center of humanity, the center piece and center point of human suffering and death. The Incarnate One, with pierced feet.

In his dying breaths, Jesus sweeps us all together for our common bonds: "Woman, here is your son," and to John, "Here is your mother" (John 19:26–27). Mother. Child. Sons. Brothers. All with toes counted by mothers. Born of the flesh, and of one flesh. Our humanity. Three crosses and God in the middle of it all.

The *Via Dolorosa*, the Way of Sorrows—and feet walking the way of suffering. Jesus is thirsty because he is dying. Jesus is dying because he is human. This is our common humanity. These feet of ours. Clay. All of us, inextricably bound by our humanity, and the human predicament, that we are subject to death. The clutch that grabs our feet at the ankles and throws us down.

We wash these feet on Maundy Thursday. A loving act of servanthood. Seeing one another as the incarnate Christ, manifest in you, and me. And a cleansing ritual preparation, for our burial.

Initiative for Prayer

Prayer as Foot Washing

This is not a Maundy Thursday ritual, but a home spa moment when you love and serve a member of your household as the Incarnate One. Prepare a basin of any kind with warm, soapy water. Prepare a pitcher of warm water. Prepare a towel or two, and a chair, and a cushion on the floor. In the simplest of ways, wash the feet of a household member, or a friend.

As you wash, contemplate the profound role our feet have in our lives.

Honor the footwork of coming and going each day, and the journey of one foot in front of another, as a routine *Via Dolorosa*. How is it that we absorb the suffering of the world as we circumnavigate the globe each day? Wash the feet as a ritual gesture of welcome and coming home, washing off, and letting go. Invite your partner to rest in knowing that the path we walk is in the company of Christ.

I am not afraid of dying. But I am afraid of death. Death has ripped me stem to stern like a grizzly, so it frightens me. An old woman took me to task when I was in my mid-twenties. She was in my Bible study class and I was teaching from 1 Corinthians. "Where, O death, is your victory? Where, O death, is your sting?" (1 Corinthians 15:55).

I thought it electrifyingly brave, Paul's mocking death. Mocking death, for thinking itself victorious, and wielding a fatal prick of poison. Personifying death. The perfect voice for taking up my lifelong exchange of enraged whispers with the bigger-than-life villain with whom I had done battle.

Speaking for myself, but with a universal air about things, I said something to the effect of "Death being the enemy." I thought it was good theology. It had certainly been my enemy. It was the truth for me. Death had surely sent God scrambling to do battle, to fight to the teeth.

She took me to task because she thinks death is a friend. The peaceful end to a long-suffering life. She nursed her aged mother through a long dementia, and then her husband was incapacitated. A wheelchair at home, and days full of the nonsense of not knowing. And she, again, waited for death, her friend. It was the first time I ever encountered such a notion. For my experience, death was the archenemy. The long-suffering diapering of my rickety grandfather, the ravages of cancer on my resplendent mother, all of it, death's wicked foreplay. The snatch-and-grab specter in the night when my grandma woke to Pappap's body, dead in the bed. My grandfather Lindberg's languishing long, and living in our home, blind, and senile, and yet grief-stricken for his lost love of fifty-six years to the grave. Death, enjoying the kill.

But it was my mother's youthful demise that first animated death, gave it a life of its own. A player on my stage, like Paul's, "O Death!" The vocative case, for direct address.

I was a toddler. Two years old, but almost three. I was dependent on her. Isn't every toddler dependent on her mother? Ours was as it should be, a naturally symbiotic relationship, and so my soul, and psyche, my existence, my real substance, was mingled with hers. When she died, she pulled me down to the grave. If she ceased to exist, did I? If she cannot see me, can I be seen? If I think I live, and breathe, and leave footprints on this earth, do I, actually? Do I have power and place? Do I matter? Am I matter? Material? Substance? Am I real?

I write about existential crisis, and I preach it, because I think everyone struggles with such existential questions. Maybe they do, maybe they don't. But I do. And this is mine: Can God forget, like my mother forgot, me? My existential crisis is tangled up with the mystery of the great deep. The water: both the womb and the grave. And what is God's place and power in it? And what, of mine? And what, of this enemy? I thought everyone wondered about death the way I do. Oh, my universal air. My walking the way of sorrows with my feet. My old friend thinks death is a friend.

This same old woman gave me a gift when I was ordained: the in-home communion kit that I still carry today. A pastoral tool for delivering the body and blood of Jesus in bread and wine to the infirm. I was nine months pregnant with Caroline, and one week overdue. When I unwrapped the package, and opened the black box, to the pristine sterling silver chalice and paten inside, I felt a snap in my side, sharp, and sudden, and my water broke. Through the night, and into the morning, I birthed my second child, a pink ribbon of a baby girl, my precious Caroline Lucille.

Mother and daughter. Symbiotic and interdependent. Again. Matter and substance. Commonality in the body, and the blood, and the little feet, with ten toes. Incarnation. Some twenty-four years later, when June rolled round once again, and fragrance of magnolia and gardenia tugged at my heart strings, and stole me away into reminiscence of birthing Caroline, I indulged my Celtic persuasion, and penned her a little blessing of the Trinity, and the water of baptism, for her birthday. "May God over the abyss, call your name out loud. May God of matter, and substance, join you on your way. May God of wind, and breath, and mist, fill you, and lift you off your feet."

Initiative for Prayer

Prayer as an Existential Crisis Challenged

Find some brown craft paper, even a few lunch bags cut length-wise into two strips each.

Using tempera paint, paint the bottom of your foot and press your foot onto the papers, making several footprints. Place the papers around the house, in different places, where you will see them from time to time. As you go about your days this week and come across your footprints, say your name out loud. Tell yourself, "She was here," and then, "I am here." Affirm your existence. Pick up the paper footprint, the evidence of your existence, and kiss it, before putting it back in place. Speak to God about yourself, in the third person, as though you are the co-creating Holy Spirit, or a caregiver for yourself. Say charming things about you. Rejoice with God in your incarnate being.

There was a garden. Eden. Water first. A dome. Roundness of belly. Full of water. Mountains and hills were brought forth when God pushed the waters back. God pushed. The waters broke. And the dry land she called: Earth.

God's birthing event. God as Mother. Earth, and clay, and breathing out, and breathing in, and Adam. Animated. Dancing feet, twirling feet, leaping, hiking, suede wrapped, booted and bare. Ten toes and counting.

A second Adam. And our common humanity. Our feet. His feet. On the ground. Of the ground. Human. This, God's finishing event, this Good Friday. God's day of rest. God's vanquishing. This creation is finished, today. Good Friday, the one day that I am not afraid of death. Because I know God is in the water, with me, and death is finished.

Initiative for Prayer

Prayer as Sculpting God as Mother

Use clay, or mud, or wet sand. In a basin or a trough, mound it like a hill, or a belly.

Cover it with water and sit in contemplation with the Divine. Imagine God pushing, laboring to birth. Lift the earth out of the water or drain the water from around the earthen material. Give God voice and welcome this earth. Name it. Say it out loud, "Earth."

Take a handful of the substance and form it into some representation of yourself, and welcome yourself as having substance and being born of God.

> In the beginning when God created the heavens and the earth, the earth was a formless void and darkness covered the face of the deep, while a wind from God swept over the face of the waters. (Genesis 1:1–2)

> On the seventh day God finished the work that he had done . . . in creation. (Genesis 2:2–3)

Jesus said, "'It is finished'" (John 19:30). The sixth word. It is finished. The sixth word from the cross on the lips of Jesus. This is that day. Good Friday is the seventh day of creation, the day God finished the work. Good Friday is God at rest. Finished and lying down. God's sabbath.

Genesis is beautiful in its symmetry and balance; the rhythm and repetition make it roll off the lips even without the book. Lovely and picturesque and full of imagery. But the creation account is, from the outset, a story about life and death, a working out of humanity's existential concern about the abyss, the formless void. The deep.

Our trouble is with the deep. Before we were brought into being there was the darkness over the water, "the face of the deep." And we wonder, can it take us back? Will the depths overcome us? What about the deep darkness? In the telling of the seven days of creation, the language is all about the deep. How the waters were separated, gathered, parted; how the darkness was set by borders, marked and measured by light, and there in the middle of it all on the sixth day, amidst the deep waters pushed back to the edges, within the changing darkness, God set God's image to walk the earth. His beloved, humankind, in male and female expression, set down in the middle of it all, on the dry land. Earth, surrounded by parted waters.

In the story, there is a preeminent darkness, and we worry about that. Can darkness take over the light? Can water swallow dry ground? Can we cease to exist? Our trouble is not about dominion and subduing the earth. Our trouble is with the deep. The water itself. The depths. The formless void. And darkness over the face of it.

Poetic images hint about the grave. Before anything was made that is, before mountains and hills and vegetation, before the dome and the lights in the sky, before humankind, there was this formless void. Light stretches to the outer limits, but nightly recurrences of darkness riddle us with primitive anxiety about the light in the sky, and our place on dry ground.

It is the kind of angst that makes the psalmist wail about dark nights, "In the night my hand is stretched out without wearying; my soul refuses to be comforted" (Psalm 77:2). "You keep my eyelids from closing; I am so troubled that I cannot speak" (Psalm 77:4).

It is our existential despair. Our nervous concern about our own existence. Matter, and substance, and the fear that we are just imagined, or invented in our own minds, or altogether absent from reality. Forgotten. Abandoned. The abyss, the formless void, the deep darkness. Death.

Our faithful poets from among the ancient Hebrew people collect our angst, and shape it for corporate tongue and gathered community. It is of such magnitude and proportion that we call it: religion. They ask the questions for us. Are God's promises at an end for all time? Has his anger shut up his compassion? Has his steadfast love ceased to exist? Can God forget?

"'It is enough; now, O Lord, take away my life'" (1 Kings 19:4). "'It is my grief that the right hand of the Most High has changed'" (Psalm 77:10). These are the dark night of the soul. The eclipse of God. The formless void. Our problem is with the deep. Eventually the prophets and poets work their way around, to rattle the mind, and pull at Moses for memory and motif of how it is, how it has been, for God and the people of God, in deep water. "When the waters saw you, O God, when the waters saw you, they were afraid; the very deep trembled. . . . Your way was through the sea, your path, through the mighty waters" (Psalm 77:16, 19). Exodus and redemption—and a way out.

God goes down into the deep water with them. Their own history. Their own saga of slavery in Egypt, and their liberation. Their own feet at the brink of plunging to their death in the depths of the Red Sea, reminds them that God himself goes down into deep water and God's presence makes a path through it. Dry ground again. They say it back to him, as worship. You, "who dried up the sea, the waters of the great deep," you "who made the depths of the sea a way for the redeemed to cross over" (Isaiah 51:10).

Our trouble is with the deep.

On the seventh day, with the taste of death in his mouth and darkness covering the earth, Jesus said, "It is finished" (John 19:30). God, down into the deep. Down to the grave. Deep into the formless void of the abyss. God laid down in the grave to make "the waters of the great deep a way for the redeemed to cross over." Creation. Redemption. Same day. One day. The seventh day. God finished the work that he did in creation, and God rested in the grave. It is Finished. This is our Sabbath rest.

Initiative for Prayer

Prayer as Symbolic Remembrance

In baptism, the water in the font is symbolic for the womb and being born by the creative acts of God. It is also the grave, symbolizing Christ lying down in the grave, and his resurrection from the tomb. In the thanksgiving over the water we say, "In it we are buried with Christ in his death. By it we share in his resurrection."[53]

Fill a bowl with seashells, or place them individually around the house, on a shelf, beside the alarm clock, on the counter near the sink, on top of a stack of books. Say Alleluia prayers, which is our song at the grave, when you see the shells here and there, as a celebration of your own resurrection. Lie down on the floor, or on a bed or a bench, or in a swimming pool if you have access to one. Ask the same creative power of God that formed you, and gave you life, to again hover over you, and call your name at the grave. And then, get up, and tell God you're coming out. Let the shells recall the deep for you. Ask God to bring life, and order, out of some deep overwhelming force in your life that threatens to pull you down. Ask God for a way through the great deep, to let you feel the deep waters tremble, because of God's presence in them. Ask God for new birth, a resurrected life, up and out of the grave. Ask Christ to share his resurrection with you. Write down what he says in your journal.

11

OPEN WATER SWIM

The sea is about being born. God, the birthing mother, moving out over the waters. We pour water in a basin and it becomes the sea itself. The face of the deep. The waters. A basin. A bowl. Like the round earth full of water before there was form. A dome.

At a baptism seminar, Anna held the bowl on her lap, a big wide bowl, circling her arms around it so that fingertips didn't really reach to touch on the other side. Arms outstretched, and fingers spread so palms braced, and balanced the weight of the water, to be for us an image of the maternal. Birth waters. Her arms around the great round waters, to let it be for us the image of the womb. Feminine. Creator God. Mother God. Birthing God. Birth waters.

When my firstborn was five months old, I remember the blissful thought in my exhaustion at three o'clock in the morning as I nursed him in the cool silence of the dark, and in my want to go back to sleep, that there was no moment so poignant as this, when I felt the weight of his body in my arms in equal portion to knowing the deep, delicious truth that I was a mother. His mother.

My babies know God by what kind of mother I have been. Their first face for God was mine. Their first voice for the divine, their first hearing God call their names? Mine. Their first experience of divine nurture was my counting of their toes and my care and tending in the nursery. My blessing and my encouragement were their way of knowing they were the apple of God's eye; or my absence was a source of their dishonor and undermined esteem.

As mother, I have failed.

So, the source of my rue is, also, the source of my delight, and my repentance is my hope for sacred rectitude, and my failing is grievous disappointment. And yet my want is fulfilled, my life complete, in the breaking waters of their birthing, and all is my source of understanding God. My motherhood. All one jumbled-up distorted tangled mess for God's untangling.

I muse at watching children, and grownups, at the beach in the summer, not just our own group, but everyone everywhere. We muse at the way we all enter the water: we run to the sea. We delight. We throw out our arms to the sides in a wide embrace. We jump around, and splash, and play, and throw ourselves in. We leap. We plunge. We immerse ourselves. I think this is one of those precious moments that J. Philip Newell longs for: a visible reality, which is the "recovery of a spirituality that is integrated with the mystery of creation."[54] The Celtic tradition, he says, "reflect[s] the desire that countless numbers of people in the Western world are becoming aware of," this reintegration, "a wholeness that will hold together their spirituality with their love of creation."[55]

My prayer for my children is that their return to the sea is their healing. Their mother found. Their geneses secured. Their epiphany, that the love of God for them is fathomless, and that God's joy in them is in equal measure to their body weight suspended and held in the mother arms of the deep salt sea. Their esteem restored, and the world's toxins purged by the saltiness, and God's raw presence. Their lives buoyed up by the joy, and delight, of God, in her birthing them. My prayer is that my children will pray the sea. That they will get in the water.

Initiative for Prayer

Play Day as Prayer

There are endless possibilities here. Go to a body of water and do something to get in it—stream, river, ocean, pool at the YMCA, anything. Swim, float, canoe, boogie board, sail, raft, fish, wade, collect tadpoles, sit on the banks of a creek and listen. Walk in heavy rain and play in the puddles. All the while, keep the motif of Nativity in your heart and mind; Nativity is the birthing of the Holy One. Imagine yourself being born of God, swimming in the prenatal waters of the divine, you, the image of God, from heaven to earth come down. You, bursting forth from the womb. You, the incarnate love of God.

Prayer as Household Chore

Wash your sheets and hang them out on the line when you know it is going to rain. Leave them out until the weather changes again, and they dry in the sun. Breathe deep, and rest in the scent of fresh rain, and the delight of smelling God. Fill a sink with suds and take your time with dishes and a child on a chair beside you. Add extra unbreakable cups and containers for pouring. Rest in the delight of God-play. Place a pitcher of fresh water, and a glass, on someone's nightstand, refill water bottles for lunch boxes, place a large shallow bowl of water outside for the birds, all with a view, and a prayer, to the whole lot of us, drinking deep for the holy joy of God's substance. Drag out the hose or the watering can, even if you don't have a garden. Spray something that needs water, fling it up overhead to make rain, wash a car or bicycle or the siding on the house. Take delight in the water, and how God in the water changes everything.

———————

A wind from God swept over the face of the waters.
(Genesis 1:2)

Dousing babies. Plunging babies into the waters of baptism. They are barely emergent from the birth waters of the womb, and here we are drenching them. A pouring, and a holy splash, so they will know that God is in the water. A pouring, and a holy splash, to wake them up. Water on them and on the rest of us with the spritzing of the aspergillum, so we will all know, in no uncertain terms, that life in this physical world is a spiritual endeavor, and that water is the substance of divine revelation. We give away all the holy secrets of our sacraments and entrust them to infants with a holy splash of water. Baptism is their first knowing of how elemental it is to find God.

Sometimes it feels like we come to church to find God. But really, we come to church to be reminded, in the sacraments, that God is to be found, out there, in the world, in all of creation, in our everyday, ordinary life. We are sent out every Sunday into the world, to go find God.

A sacrament is an outward and visible sign of inward and spiritual grace. Every time we eat the bread of Holy Eucharist, we hold the truth that God is in us. Every drink from the chalice makes us know that God is found in the goodness of the earth, and every table becomes a place to feast on God. Whether a picnic on a blanket, or waiting tables in a café, God is present, and the bread and wine at Eucharist makes me remember it. So, I can go out, and find God, in my life in the world.

This material life we live in the world is all about finding, meeting, experiencing, and being surprised by God. Sacraments make us know that God is right in front of us, around us, under us, in us. We go to church, and we sing hymn, and anthem, and play trumpet, and woodwinds in a great pipe organ, because we need to be reminded that God is in our very breath. We make music because we need to be reminded that the invisible breeze that makes trees dance and messes up our hair is God playing with us. Every gasp, every whistle, every shout is a moment of breathing God.

We light the Paschal candle at baptism. It is the outward and visible sign that tells us the truth about the Christ. That the incarnate light of the world has overcome death and the grave. Light shines in the darkness and darkness cannot overcome it. We light the paschal candle, and torches for Gospel procession, and pillars on our altar on Sundays, because of the truth is that God is in the fire. That God is the Light. Our torches on brass lamp stand and acolyte tended, remind us that God is out there in the fire light of every hearth. And that the flicker of a night light on a child's bed table helps us find God in the dark. Every horizon by morning, and every cook stove in the kitchen, make us know that God is at hand.

We are a sacramental people. The outward and visible stuff makes us recognize the presence of God. The things we do in church, the things we call sacraments and sacramental acts, substantiate for us that God is out there in the world, and that is where we will find him. In the sacrament of baptism, God is in the water. God is in the pourable, splashable, swimmable, drinkable water, of all creation.

God is in the water of baptism. It heightens our expectation, and we go out seeking God in flowing fountains, salt or fresh, drizzling rain, the crashing coast of the Pacific Northwest, or the frozen cap of the Antarctic. God is in the water; you can find God, even in your own bathtub. Baptism is a floodgate to knowing God. The headwaters. Just the beginning. The font. It is your invitation. Full of possibility and promise.

Initiative for Prayer

Prayer as a Ritual Practice with a Holy Relic

When we bless the water at baptism, we are saying two things. One, it is good. Two, God is in it. That is why we call it holy water: because God is in it.

Bring a little bottle to church for the next upcoming baptism celebration. Dip into the big bowl at the font. Take it home. Sit in a quiet place and hold the water; think about your home, your household, your life, and the people in it with you. Sprinkle the holy water around. Bless the places and the people with the God-water.

Here are some more suggestions: Consecrate a place with it, a place where you have known God's presence, or want to. Re-consecrate a place where something has gone wrong. Sprinkle the ground where you have buried a pet. Cross your child's forehead with the water and say, "Remember your Baptism, you are 'marked as Christ's own, forever.'"[56] Cross your own forehead with the water to remember your baptism, and that you are born of God, a child of the Most High. Splash a little holy water in the tub, and get in. Laugh a little, or giggle, if it tickles you. Shake some over your bed and consecrate your love life. Celebrate that God is love. Water play. You will find God in all of it, because God is in the water. Make things new. Make the life you want. Claim your place as holy. This is your prayer. Pray the sea.

I have a new hobby—the outdoor triathlon, which combines swimming, running, and riding a bike. Kim and Joey took me for my first open water training swim in the marina cove, the backwaters of the Chattahoochee River. It was summertime, but it was early morning, and the water was cold. I was riddled with anxiety about all of it. I was stressed about my athletic friends, both confident and faster swimmers than I, and then there was my usual sense of not fitting in with athletes.

The water itself was eerie. Unknown creatures that also swim in the lake, plankton and strange green filigree scraping along my belly and lacing the skin under my suit. And I was afraid. It was barely light. The water was dark. I had to put my face in it, and I couldn't see and I couldn't breathe. It was a complete unknown. And then, after one full lap, past five wide-spread buoys, down to the pontoon boat and back to the dock, it all changed.

My athletic friends became just companions, company in the water. I became captivated by the water itself, and the beauty and sensual pleasures. The moon enormous in the sky, the mist hovering over the water, the subtle changes in the light, a slight sunrise, and the shoreline on the other side. Swimming endlessly without banking off the ends of the pool, and the cool temperatures, became invigorating and refreshing. The slow illumination of my arms under the water was mesmerizing, as though I was seeing them for the first time. Quiet consistent lapping sounds of the water as it parted about my body. All of it was exquisite. I felt like I could swim all day, and my triathlon swimsuit, which resembles a 1920s version of spandex, looked like I had rolled in the mud. And I felt fully alive. I had never imagined such a rich outdoor life.

For the rest of the day, I kept telling everybody about the swim, but I could see in their eyes that they just didn't get it. They seemed more taken with the stupidity of getting in the water of the Chattahoochee River. I'm not sure you can get it if you've never done it. The only way I got it was by getting in the water, and swimming.

God is in the ordinary stuff of ordinary life. The ordinary water of baptism is sacramental, it is the outward and visible sign that our whole selves are sustained, and suspended, in God. It lends the candor of seeing our own skin as if for the first time, and the beauty of subtle illumination and gradual coming into light. It tells us the inward and spiritual truth, that the entirety of our being is immersed in God, our souls buoyed up by God's unfathomable depths, and immediate presence, and that we ourselves in our bodies are the pure, and holy, illuminated, delight of God.

God in the water is an exotic surprise. God, exquisite and captivating. Mesmerizing in beauty and pleasure, and not altogether predictable with subtle changes in light, and a slow dawning brilliance of ourselves. Immersion in God is full body. It is fairly difficult to explain the euphoria of God in an open water swim. The only way to know is to get in. To let go of everything that keeps you on the shoreline. Just get in and swim. Get in, and take all the gripping fears, anxieties, and discomforts about God, and the water, and get in.

Initiative for Prayer

Prayer as Getting In

Go for a swim. Get in the water.

12

MISTLETOE

A dear old saint of a woman is grieving her dying husband. She loved him her whole life long, since she was a girl of fourteen, and now she is eighty-two. Ever-vibrant, with delicate features and striking white locks and red lipstick, poetry on her tongue, and humor in her eyes. She can't stop touching him; feeling him present in the body, when he has lost presence of mind to a bleeding stroke, the culmination of a distancing journey begun with Parkinson's disease.

"He isn't there," she says. "Just for a moment, now and then." But she touches him. Pats him, holds his hand, comforts him, wipes his chin. She weeps, and laughs, and weeps. And weeps. And she remembers funny stories with him.

She offers a narthex confession in jest, that she is guilty of the sin of worshiping him, adoring him, loving him more than God. And I, in a narthex absolution, swipe her brow, and commend her for grasping the deep mysteries of the Incarnation. How can we know the intimate love of God, the company of the Trinity, the delight of the Companionship, the standing at the foot of the cross, the shifting bone of the Nativity, without the physical love of the image of God? "Annie," I said, "loving him more than God? Loving him *is* loving God." Passion. Abandon. Veneration. These are her delight in the beloved Christ. O Come, let us adore him.[57]

She is wry. She already knows all that. She is being dutiful to the priest. But I am not thwarted. I say it for the pleasure, we both like hearing it. For I have found my beloved. And I know new mysteries.

Initiative for Prayer

Prayer as Creating a Love Collage

Cut out a construction paper heart. Write over and over on the heart, "O Come, Let Us Adore Him." Fill it in, write it fancy, use block printing, write big and write small, just scroll, scroll, scroll the words on the heart. Now consider the people you love and adore. Think of their faces, their ways, their voices, their sense of humor, their unique gestures. Thank God for letting you love. Let yourself love and adore them. Cut out some pictures of these people and paste them onto the heart. If that's too cumbersome, write their names and some of the things you love about them. Add some glitter, sequins, or gilt from wrapping. Recognize the Divine in them.

Hold this heart in your hands and meditate on the little Bible verse that says: "God is love" (1 John 4:8). Let divine love take root in your heart. Meditate on the love of God. Celebrate your love for God, and the gift of Incarnate Presence in the people around you.

The physical absence of my mother has borne my need for the physical presence of God. I have to find God in the flesh. The longing is too much. I couldn't let my children cry themselves to sleep when they were babies. I couldn't bear it. No matter that some books said it was best for them, nor if the doctors recommended it, or friends and family testified to the method and maternal wisdom of it. I couldn't do it. Their cries conjured visceral experience of my own abandonment. I nurtured my own soul by picking them up; their consolation, mine. My relief. Mine. They know still what they learned in the nursery; that their cries of abandonment batter me and make me dance like a puppet on a string. Me their marionette.

When my Caroline eased from infancy into toddlerhood, with her very early grasp of language, I would lean over her crib, pat her back, and sing softly until I thought she drifted off to sleep, then slowly I would stop the singing, stop the patting, but stand there motionless for a bit before tiptoeing away. Just as I tried to slip away, she would lift her head, turn it my way, and say, "pat," and I would pat. And then she would do it again, and say, "sing," and I would sing. And there we would be in a singing, patting, lullaby moment, of Madonna and Child, ever treasuring the irretrievable moments of our creche.

I nursed the Christ at my breast as did the saints in rapturous visions. These three of me, born of a woman. Bathing the Christ. Feeding the Christ. Calling them blessed. They are God in human form to me. God, in a body. Real, and substantial, such that I can touch, pat, bathe, hold, feed, tend, and kiss. Form and substance. Matter. Born of a woman, the Christ to me. For me.

> According to legend, Brigid was the midwife and wet nurse of the Christ Child. She is described as the barmaid at the inn in Bethlehem where Mary and Joseph seek shelter. There is no room at the inn but Brigid provides them with space in the stable. At the moment of the birth, Brigid midwives the Christ Child and then suckles him at her breast.[58]

Little liturgical gestures please me because I can kiss the Christ. The cross at the neck of my stole, the corporeal on the altar that held his body and blood that linger still with the scent of wine and scrap of bread. I need, want, love the physical gesture. Expression. It brings me Christ. It satisfies me with devotion. Bow, genuflect, cross my body, thump my breast. All manifestations of my God-love.

I lie down with my Christ at night, in my prayers and in the embrace of my beloved, my legs intertwined with his. The pillow crunched under my head, and the fetal curl to spoon his sacred body. The heat of feathered bed and human form. God in a body.

In *The Book of Creation*, J. Philip Newell shares a beautiful Celtic night prayer, which was included in the *Carmina Gadelica*. Prayers of lying down with the Trinity heighten our awareness of holy sleep, and the presence of God in the night hours. Praying God with us in our rest reminds us that rest, too, is sacred. Resting with God, and just as God rested, on the seventh day.

> I lie down this night with God,
> And God will lie down with me;
> I lie down this night with Christ,

And Christ will lie down with me;
I lie down this night with Spirit,
And the Spirit will lie down with me;
God and Christ and the Spirit
Be lying down with me.[59]

All human flesh is holy, and it changes the way I see you. If I cup the chin of one who weeps, I catch the tears of Christ. Water births us God, and every baptism is a Nativity. The Christ lifted up out of the water and dripping. God in a body, for our falling in love, and for our kissing.

———————

Initiative for Prayer

Prayer as the Practice of Holy Kissing

Give yourself the opportunity to kiss as an expression of your love for God. Choose something that has meaning to you, such as a cross on a chain, a religious medal, a piece of fabric, a seashell or stone from a pilgrimage, a picture, a lichen-covered branch, anything that brings you a sense of the Holy One. Place it where you will see it in the course of your day. When you see it, pick it up and kiss it and allow your soul to open to the physical expression of love for the Divine.

———————

Far up in the branches of a live oak clung a bunchy cluster of mistletoe, big as a bushel basket, and loaded with sticky pearls. We wanted some because Christmas is for kissing. So, the three of us set about our mission. Boy, does mistletoe cling to its limbs. First, we threw things. Heavy-heeled boots and shoes. Golf balls, baseballs, and a few rocks. Then we tried a bow and arrow, scattering like mice to dodge the descending ammunition until we were exhausted. But finally, we lobbed a whole ball of heavy twine up and over the branch. Holding on to one end, and dangling the other, we tied a long walking stick horizontally; swift yanks on the rope, pulley like, in see-saw fashion whacking the airborne shrub, and attracting all sorts of curious attention, until branch by branch, we had our harvest.

Ribboned, and hung on the porch, in the doorways, and carried in hand when it was useful for chasing someone. Mistletoe, for arriving home in love, and going out in love. And all around the house, a bundled love game, because Christmas is for kissing.

The Feast of the Incarnation. It is all about God in a body, for love.

A catechist surprised me one day. We were leading a seminar together, preparing parents and families for baptism. So, of course, we were talking about sacrament. The outward and visible signs that tell us what is true about God. True, about inward and spiritual realities.

"So, what about the signs?" I asked. "What are they?"

The group was reeling them off: "Well, there's water, and the Paschal candle, fire and flame, light, and oil for anointing, the white garment," and the catechist piped up, "And the kiss."

There is no kiss at baptism. I felt myself flush with the realization that people watch more closely in church than I thought they did. I felt myself seen, spied on almost, because she saw. And she was right. I do kiss the babies when I baptize them.

Of course, we kiss babies, the precious swaddled bundles of joy all in white linen. But there's another reason. The liturgical kiss. The sacramental kiss. The outward and visible sign that tells the truth of spiritual things. That God from heaven has to earth come down. God in human form: all human flesh is holy because God inhabits it. So, there, in my arms, is my chance to kiss the infant Christ: this boy-child a God-bearer, this baby-girl, the Holy One incarnate.

Kissing God. Liturgical kisses and falling in love. The drama of devotion. The rituals of affection. The Feast of the Incarnation. God in a body for loving, for lavishing. Lavish the Divine, because without a body incarnate, we have only mystery, and metaphor, when there is, or can be, the thrilling pleasure of God in a body, all around us.

Initiative for Prayer

Prayer as Sacramental Kissing

Mistletoe is a year-round green growing airborne plant. No matter the time of year, see if you can find some mistletoe and harvest it from the branches of a tree. If this is too difficult, simply choose some other greens like boxwood or rosemary. Tie a ribbon around the bunch of greens. In a playful gesture with someone who is your familiar, hold the greenery above his or her head. Choose one of these sentences to say or make up something that is true for you.

"You are the Holy One to me."

"You are my God-bearer."

"You are the beloved Christ to me."

"You are the beautiful face of God to me."

And then, of course, deliver a kiss to the forehead. As a dinner table fun time, exchange the dinner time prayer for a pass-around of the love bundle, with one of the phrases listed above, accompanied with a forehead kiss. Each one, kiss one.

There is a love note in the holy books of Moses. An ancient scroll within a scroll, five little verses in Deuteronomy. A tiny piece of parchment pulled out from all the rest. A sacred truth, written down, and rolled up, and tucked into crevices of door posts, garden gates, and in the human heart. A love note. A passion spoken with all the romance of Shakespeare and written with all the charm of Dickens. God-love. A word of holy want that tells it all.

The Shema. Divine fire. The want of God for you. God enticing you to love. God impassioned, beckoning, imploring you, to a divine love affair, with the Holy One.

The Shema. "Hear, O Israel: The Lord is our God, the Lord alone. You shall love the Lord your God with all your heart, and with all your soul, and with all your might" (Deuteronomy 6:4–5). God-love. There in Deuteronomy. Our sacred sonnet. Our holy love poem. The Divine, luring for want of us to love God. It says to write these love words on a tiny script, and then tuck it in your heart, and wear it all around. Speak of it in whispers when you lie down, and wake with the joy of it when you rise up. Wear the love. Put it on. Dress up. Adorn yourself. Wear the love words on your hand, wind them around your wrist. Wrap them up your arm, that your every touch, and all your reaching, will be laced with the love of God. Write the words, and bind the love to your forehead, a headdress for your beloved. Wear them like jewels upon your brow, that your every thought, and wildest imaginations, will be ignited by the holy fire of divine love.

It's all about the love. Whole body devotion for the love of God. Attach it to your fence post, and to the gate, and the door frames of your house, a kind of mistletoe overhead, that you might go out in love, and come home, in love. Get all tangled up, and overwhelmed, with the love of God. It's all right there in the tiny little piece of Deuteronomy.

The Shema. That's what it's all about. It's all about the love. Falling in love with God. All the rest of it, the law and the prophets, poetry and promise, command and decree, sage and saga? All of it, every bit of it, is right there in Deuteronomy 6, a heart, soul, mind, and strength kind of falling in love with God.

Christmas Eve has a way of enticing the throngs to come out late at night. The Feast of the Nativity, and we all want this God-love, this enticing Word, the sacred sonnet. The love note of God's Deuteronomic luring has taken form, and substance, and the love of God has become human flesh.

The truth of the Incarnation is a woman great with child whose time has come to be delivered. Birth pangs and shifting bones in a bed of hay, a baby wrapped in swaddling clothes, a trough, and manger for a crib. God has been born, and we are falling in love. We come in these wee hours of birth to see the mystery of God made flesh, and all humanity hallowed.

The truth of the Incarnation means that every baptism is a Nativity, a birthing of the Holy One. The Christ, emerging from the birth waters of baptism, drenched from the womb. You, the Christ. Me, the Christ. God in human form. The Christ in infant form. We kiss the babies because we are falling in love with God. The infant in white linen, and lace, and doused forehead, bears God for me, and I cannot resist the kiss.

Babies make us know it is easy to fall in love. We are love-struck at their birthing. We wrap our arms around to hold them close, we sway, and swoon. We become contemplatives in a flash, gazing for love, marking and memorizing the twists, and turns, the details of fingerprint and follicle. Our piety exceeds the saints' capacity for devotion. Instant mystics, the lot of us. Babies do it to us. Cooing, and crooning, and tripping over ourselves, for the sacred swaddled. We make shrines of tiny footprints and locks of hair because we fall in love.

It was happening for Mary in these pages of the gospel that tell her story. The shepherds rushed in, and angels sang their chorus. But Mary, it says, "treasured all these words and pondered them in her heart" (Luke 2:19). Oh, but to embrace the sweet Divine. It makes us full with want, and we stretch for language and use the King's English for such a story, because suddenly we want to use words like "abiding" and "haste," and we know what it means to be sore afraid. We want sonnet-worthy rhythm and cadence to our speech. Lovely words and turns of phrase, and mystery-laden beauty that makes us hush and bow. The fragrance of divine love in frankincense, and the fire of divine heat in myrrh. We swoon in this manger-stall, and we fall for God.

Jesus is love incarnate, and we venture out in the midnight hour on Christmas Eve, because we want to fall in love. With liturgical kissing, and Deuteronomic mistletoe, we give ourselves over, and dare God to stir our passions with the high romance of Christmas. The peel of church bells, and tipping joy with eggnog, the magic of midnight and candlelight. Our hearts are on fire, and ready for an announcement: "For unto you is born this day" (Luke 2:11 KJV).

And Christmas is our kissing.

———

Initiative for Prayer

Prayer as a Ritual of Coming and Going in Love

Purchase a stoup, or create one, and fix it to your household doorway. It's simply a container for holy water, a miniature font or bowl that is flat on one side so that it can attach to the door frame. If you don't have a cat or dog, you could just place a bowl at the threshold on the floor. Fill it with holy water that you scooped up from the last baptism.

Each time you come or go through the doorway, touch your fingers to the holy water, and swipe it on your forehead, or lips, or hand, or wrist, or heart. Hear God beckoning to you with that sacred love poem in Deuteronomy. See if you can practice the same divine passion by answering in kind. See if you can respond to God with the words: I love you with all my heart, all my soul, all my mind, and all my strength (Deuteronomy 6:5).

———

PART IV

God in Air

*To include breeze, breath, sky,
drafts, vibration, oxygen, heavens,
atmosphere, play, air current,
music, wind, humidity, and scent.*

And God said, "Let there be a dome in the midst of the waters, and let it separate the waters from the waters." So God made the dome and separated the waters that were under the dome from the waters that were above the dome. And it was so. God called the dome Sky. And there was evening and there was morning, the second day. (Genesis 1:6–8)

We were driving from Oregon to Georgia on a gradual diagonal from west to east. I had previously been in only three of the states we traveled through. Just the ends. Oregon, Tennessee, and Georgia. I had heard of views where earth meets sky at every one of the 360 degrees of the horizon, but I had never seen it. It had never occurred to me that mountains, hills, and forests block your view. I always thought they were the view. It never occurred to me that sky could be seen by looking straight ahead. Pittsburgh was all mountains and valleys, everywhere. To see the sky, we had to look up. Hence, the dome.

The dome is not water. It is the separation between the waters, the space in-between. The dome is not earth, though it needs the matter and substance of the earth, one a container for the other, and together they are the whole of creation: the heavens and the earth, the complete and finished work of God. One is not complete without the other. Nor is the dome to be confused with fire, by which we see or are illumined. Those are the lights that God placed in the dome, a greater one and a lesser one—the sun, and the moon—to be the lamps for day and night. God called the dome Sky.

The high crosses scattered on the horizon of Celtic landscapes bid us to get outside, out in the dome, arms outstretched like the cross, and subject to the "wild wind carrying the incipient life of the universe in its wings."[60] The crosses reached and stretched, called people to gather around them, and stood as visual reminders of God in creation, and creating still. "The early Celtic Church was characterized by patterns of worship and prayer under the open skies . . . in wild, exposed sites . . . Earth, sea and sky, rather than enclosed sanctuaries, were the temple of God [pointing] to the conviction that the holy mystery of God is unbounded."[61]

We see, breathe, take flight, and lie down at night, in the context of the dome. We are ever and always sleeping or waking, present to and stirring through the dome, while never actually seeing it. The dome is as ethereal as the element we call air, the element that breathes, sways, inspires, fills, moves, lifts, and gives us life. Air is the element that is seen only by what it animates, like the hair on your arm, the leaves on a tree, or Adam, when Adam became a living being. We can see the air by how it takes a shape, in a balloon or in a lung. We can smell it, by its lifting of a scent, and wafting it our way, or we can hear it by its rapid vibration with hummingbird wing or violin quartet. We feel it on our skin when someone whispers in our ear. Always, its effects, rather than the thing itself. Dust mites, in a shaft of light, float. Such is God when we find God in the elements of creation, and that's what makes us call air: Holy Spirit.

Air is every moment, our holy necessity. God, from one breath to the next without thought, or intent, the dynamic of inhale, and exhale, a sort of Holy Spirit resting presence. God is the effervescence in a toast, a sort of Holy Spirit joy. God, the encapsulated fullness of a child's bubble-blowing, or the lift of a dragonfly wing, a sort of Holy Spirit playing. God is the saying of our names out loud when we are brought into being, a sort of Holy Spirit animation. We gasp for air in our birthing, and in our dying, a gasping for God, a cry for Holy Spirit, and extreme unction—our subconscious want for God. This constant rest in Holy Presence, this laughter, this joy, this play, and our coming to life with Holy Spirit. Newell calls this air, wind, sky, Holy Spirit, the "wildness of God"[62] that brought all things into being by wind, over the mighty waters of Genesis 1. We can expect a similar kind of turbulence, he says, when we exercise creativity in our own lives. The wildness of God that is "unrestrainable."[63]

I can see God when I look at you because Holy Spirit animates you, and if you dance or jump or lie perfectly still, I can see what God looks like at rest and play. I can hear yet another unheard nuanced voice of God because you speak out loud, and God is the voice and breath within you, uttered now. I can even find God in my dog's barking, if I pay attention to that voice, that sound, that excitement. And listen.

The poet who penned Psalm 104 says that God wears light as his cloak and stretches out the sky for a tent. If we can see sky, then we know we are in God's tent; we are at home, and God is at hand. Vistas. The broad expanse makes me breathless with Holy Presence and elated about the ridiculous blatancy of God's omniscience. From now on, whenever I engage my Celtic practice of praying the sky, I will think of that holy vastness, and me inside of it. Me inside the Holy Dome of God.

My Nana lived one hundred feet from a dead end, which dropped in what seemed, as a child, to be a cliff at the end. A steep valley is all it was really, not a cliff. When we heard a train's whistle everybody scrambled to race down to the end of the street to press against the guard rail and watch the train. We counted cars. How long was the train? Where had it been, and where was it going? Cars with a harvest of coal from inside the earth, tankers of oil from under the sea, shipping containers from faraway lands, and box cars with the mystery, and intrigue, about the possibility of hoboes inside. All the world in bits and pieces. We watched down over the cliff.

But I had never seen whole trains except in miniature at the Carnegie Science Center and under our Christmas tree at home. Platforms with papier-mâché mountains and spongey trees, and something called HO scale. Otherwise, I had seen trains only in parts, dashing before my eyes at the intersection one gigantic car at a time, in and out of tunnels, around the bend, over railroad trestles, over the river, and out of sight again. But there they were, conductor to caboose, whole trains within view on our diagonal drive from Oregon. Whole trains at a distance, hundreds of cars, and stretching for miles, like a glorious never-before-seen creature caught sunning itself, thinking it was alone. Awe and marvel. Idaho. Wyoming. Nebraska. Illinois. Stretches of the horizon where you could see the vast expanse.

Perspective, length, and breadth change everything when it comes to praying. What we can see begs the question of what we can't see. So, praying God in the element of air becomes a form of trusting that there is some unknown piece or unseen part, which if we could see or know, might change everything, but which also lies within the mystery of the vast expanse of the Holy Dome. Vision. Perspective, and seeing the whole, because I am within the dome, and the sky contains it all. And I breathe it in. And I am present to the Presence. The Unseen.

There is a clearing of the air quality to prayer when we raise a compromised holy voice in supplication, a breathing out of confession, a breathing in of absolution. The divine-laced wind that clears the air with the holy voice of restoration, reconciliation, forgiveness, and absolution, when the holy voice in another pronounces it. You are forgiven; I forgive you.

We co-opt God by the misuse of the holy voice we call our own when we wield it as weapon, to cut, injure, dispense cruelty. We ignore God, and silence holy speech, because it was spoken from the powerless, or the small, or it was uttered by the aged. We refuse God when we don't want to hear a different voice, an irrelevant voice, or one that rose as protest from the condemned, the caged, the foreign tongue, the pestering toddler. When we are all work, and no play, refuse to sing, to proclaim praise, to shout, and laugh, and whistle, too, we sin against ourselves. A kind of denying our holy animation. Or when we remain silent, and suffer abuse, because we cannot let the sound of our God-voice blurt out for our own self-defense, and we die a thousand deaths.

With soot stuck in the grooves of my fingerprints on Ash Wednesday, I press ashes to foreheads to remind us of the truth about our mortality, our made-of-the-earth quality of our selves, and our propensity for dying. But, more so, to remind me of the truth that I have learned about God from the wind: animation. Life for the lifeless form. Wind for the music in a pipe, for the wings of a bird to soar. My memory is stirred, and my hope is roused. Ashes for remembering. Ashes to remember being formed, and shaped in God's hand, and my mother's domelike holy womb for bone and marrow. Ashes to remember the gasp for breath in birthing, and God's breathing me into being for my animation, when God first said, "Ruth," out loud. This swipe of ash, so I can stand at the grave in hope that I will be formed again, and gasp again at God's breath for my resurrection, when he calls my name, and cries in a loud voice, "Come out" (John 11:43). What I have learned from the earth about being human, and my dying a thousand deaths, is informed by what I have learned about God from the air. Breath. And life. Animas. God's spirit. God's play. God so easily, delightfully, breathing, speaking, rattling the leaves, with calling my name. For Resurrection. And for life, everlasting, and abundant.

With the amount of time I keep company with the dead, one of these days I figure I'll get to be there when it happens. When the wind of God sweeps through the place, and dry bones live again. They will, in fact, get up and twirl about. I saw it start once, and it made me laugh, and want to dance a jig. I was preparing the cremains of a Navy pilot for his interment in the memorial garden. As I jostled them from the plastic container and into the linen duffle, the wind swept through and lifted him into the air in a twirl. He, a Navy pilot with decorated wings of his own, took to the wind like a natural, as if he was ready and waiting for his final flight, to dance his Alleluia dance in the burial grounds.

13

PAVILION FOR PLAY

In the house where I grew up, we had a music room. Music was, to us, what play sounded like. Two pump organs, a baby grand piano that gave way to an upright for the conservation of space, and eventually a small pipe organ. An old autoharp leaned on a chair rail ledge. During our school years, trumpet, coronet, piccolo, and flute made their debuts. There was always a metronome somewhere, with a sliding weight.

We called it the music room at our house, some households call theirs the playroom, or perhaps the keeping room or living room. Or there's the playground at the schoolhouse if there is no room at all, but somewhere we make the space to play. Wisdom says this about her role with God in the creation of the world:

> When he set the boundaries for the seas; and settled law to the waters, that they should not pass their coasts. When he weighed the foundations of the earth; I was making all these things with him. And I delighted by all days, and played before him in all time, and I played in the world; and my delight is to be with the sons and daughters of men. (Proverbs 8:29–31 WYC)

The Spirit of Wisdom, at play. The third person of the Trinity, frolicking. It seems that play is rooted in the divine companionship, and in the creative process, and requires a certain elixir of safety and abandon. A certain amount of boundary for letting go enough to discover that abandon gives way to rapture. It is our song, and our dance, our getting caught up with God. It is our shortness of breath. Our pant. It is the head thrown back in laughter or delight. What is laughter but a person's whole being expressing delight by syncopated breath, and wild alterations of pitch?

The Holy Spirit in wind, and breath, is our holy gift of play. God. In the air we breathe.

The place of real abandon for me, that space for play, the place that served up that perfect elixir of safety and abandon, was my grandmother's house. She made time for children. We whistled to the birds from the porch glider and they answered. My sister and I shopped for groceries from her spice pantry when we played house and walked our babies in a wicker carriage with iron wheels. Before recycling was chic and eco-friendly, she stashed cardboard, foil wrappers, and all sorts of string, twine, and packaging, in the end cupboard of her dining room buffet, which was actually in her big eat-in kitchen. What better place to keep the art supplies? Button boxes, marbles in cans, along with Chinese checkers, Scrabble, dominoes, tempera, watercolors, and made-up spelling bees. She played canasta nightly with Great-grandma Birdie when it came time for us to go to bed.

She had a song in her voice when she called my name. Her breath smelled like gingersnaps, and she swayed when she walked. She would un-hook her hose from their garters, and let them slide down comfortably, heaping up around each ankle. My Grandma Evans was Play incarnate, my Holy Spirit, in woman with the sensible lace-up black leather shoes with a stout high heel. She was air for me.

Benno has her same soul. He is all around, through and through, the invitation to play. My muse. My elixir. Elixir is defined as "an alchemical preparation to be capable of prolonging life or of transmitting base metals into gold."[64] And so it is with him, for me. God playing with us. God's Holy Spirit at play, transmitting base metals into gold.

We sing because we cannot resist God's residing, stirring, delighting presence in our souls. We are, all of us, always, continually under God's holy sway. God in air. How plentiful the common sparrow taking flight; a pigeon in the alleyway gutters, roosting at the edge of a house; trash drifting on a breeze; sails, flapping in the wind. God's Spirit is the wind that makes the lilt in an oboe, or lifts a kite to the sky, or sets a bamboo stand to singing. The windpipe, our instrument for sounding God's presence within us.

Worship is the formal event of God's people at play. The playground, the swing set and slide, and the great pipes of a Flentrop organ. The swell. A clarinet. A flute. Bassoon and trumpet notwithstanding. All of these, one in the same; God's Holy Spirit in wind and breath. We worship. We lift our voice in praise, and make our alleluias, and risk a certain holy rapture. And in it, we are God's sophisticated children playing.

Initiative for Prayer

Prayer as Play

Playing may be our most important spiritual initiative because it is the stuff of worship. The Holy Spirit is the source of whim, fancy, and curiosity. Abandon. Letting go and exploration. Delight. Ecstasy. Rapture. And finding intimacy with God. Experiment with play as prayer. Experiment with music and sound. Experiment with God as Holy Spirit and wind. Sing. Better yet: dance. It's feasible, that if we are people who are filled with God's Holy Spirit, that everything we do in life can be approached with the spirit of play.

Here are some ideas to get you started. Roll the dice to see who does the dishes, or on a Saturday, make a list of chores numbered one to six, and roll the dice to see which chore comes next. Play hide and seek to wonder about God playing with us. Dance. Roll up the rug and delay dinner until everyone is readjusted after a rough day. Sit on a swing, and swing, on your front porch, playground, or someone's front yard. Feel the Holy Spirit in your hair. Feel the changes in your body, torso, mind, and perspective, and the changing sensation of gravity as the swing lifts you through the air. Build a castle in the sand box, and see God drawing the circumference of the great deep or the height of the mountains.

A word about play. Don't just watch others play; play. And when you play, if playing with your children, avoid giving instruction, or teaching them. Just enter into it as best you can as a partner, using your imagination and spirit of abandon.

Prayer as Body Sculpture

Read Proverbs 8 and playact yourself as Wisdom. Play your way to accompanying God in the work of creation. Open yourself to delight. What would Wisdom wear? What would Wisdom say? What postures would Wisdom take?

If you're trying this with a larger group, select several verses of Proverbs 8 and create still-life body sculptures for a gallery. Each group of four or five creates a still-life sculpture of their appointed verse, using one or more members of the small group for the clay. The rest of the group as the sculptors, consider what facial expression Wisdom might have in the eyes, the mouth, the position of the head, and sculpt your human clay partners to take that expression. Consider the arms, and legs, and torso, to depict the meaning and feeling of the verse you've been given. When each group has finished, the sculptors get to walk through the gallery to see the other sculptures. When all have had time, change places so that the players in the still-life sculptures can enjoy the walk through, too.

Prayer as Experiment with
Music and Sound: Whistling

Use your whistler in a daily way, for at least a week. Whistle and make up a tune, so everyone else will hear the song in your heart. On a day when there isn't a song there, your whistle will lend one to you. Let it put one there on a dreary day or low moment in an afternoon. Whistle as experiment with the expression of emotion: whistle humor, whistle loneliness, whistle confusion, whistle invitation, whistle grief, whistle surprise, whistle awe and wonder, whistle work, whistle expectation. You get the idea.

Prayer as Experiment with
Music and Sound: Drumming

Percussion instruments. Explore the kitchen. Pull out a variety of implements. Pots and pans, oatmeal boxes, plates, dog food bag, wooden spoons, wire whisks, spatulas. Now, drum. Experiment with beat, sound, pitch, rhythm, and vibration. These are all components of music, and reside at the core of our physical and spiritual existence. Even the piano is considered a percussion instrument, because the little felted hammers inside strike the strings, and the vibration makes a note.

In the beginning . . . a wind from God swept over the face of the waters. (Genesis 1:1–2)

Jesus ... was baptized ... [a]nd just as he was coming up out of the water, he saw the heavens torn apart and the Spirit descending like a dove on him. (Mark 1:9–11)

On a balmy winter Saturday late one February, Benno and I, along with various offspring and neighborhood children, spent the day together at our house. A slight off-and-on drizzle kept us inside, but we had the doors open to ward off cabin fever. So, we thought it would be entertaining to make a tent. Not just a blanket draping from a table to the floor for everyone to crawl under, but a huge tent with lots of panels, big enough to house sofa and fireplace. In fact, as we built, it got so big we started calling it a pavilion.

Sheets, and tablecloths, corners bound with rope, suspended from the railing in the loft high over the living room, other panels reaching overhead from the loft as far as the mantle across the room, and more. Side walls, strung and moored at door frames, pillar, and post, with extra nails hammered into windowsills for cleats. You can do that in a 1920s bungalow. With a few bandanas, and scarves, clothespinned here and there, we filled in all the gaps. We read stories, and played games, and ate lunch on trays in our tent, and cut poster board stars, and a crescent moon to dangle with needle and thread from the mantle.

Then, without a moment's notice, the sky darkened and the temperature dropped. A storm whipped up, and a powerful wind blew through the house, and suddenly we were on a ship riding the high seas, sails flapping, sheets snapping, exciting everyone to start running about. We heard ourselves calling out with words like "Hoist," "Ahoy," and "Matey," not knowing if we were pirates or drunken sailors, but we were alive, and spoke in a new language with an accent, and we were seafarers on a ship, and we were definitely going somewhere.

Initiative for Prayer

Prayer with Tents and Scarves

Gather swathes of fabric for makeshift tents. This may be a sheet strung from the mantel, or railing, or between the bed and the dresser, or a scarf simply stretched overhead for a moment, by the strength of your own two arms. With imaginative prayer and contemplation, pray God as wind. Get inside the tent or under the scarf. Imagine God. Imagine the fabric as the heavens twirling about. Stretch it out overhead. Imagine the scarf as the whole sky, a dome, for God's tent. Ask to feel God, and to be swept up into the heart of God.

Prayer with Tents and Scarves: Imaginative Prayer, Intercession, and Petition

Get in the tent and ponder perspective. Ponder your perspective as compared to God's. If the heavens are to God as this tent is to you, what is God's perspective of things; what is yours? What does this have to offer you? Where do you need vision and clarity and perspective? Ask for it. Write what you hear in your journal.

———

God is made known in the wind. Genesis is the story of God's long, slow incarnation. God becoming flesh, not just in human being, but God being made manifest in all creation. God known. God revealed. God visible in tree, and brook, and coal in the caverns of the earth. When "the earth was a formless void and darkness covered the face of the deep . . . a wind from God swept over the face of the waters" (Genesis 1:1–2). A hovering. A brooding. Wind that becomes breath, breath that becomes a voice, voice with vowel sounds and consonants. Words that call things into being. Elephant. Cypress. Polliwog. Brindle boxer and cocker spaniel. Birth, and creation, and something of God revealed in everything, and inviting you to see. To pay attention. To listen. To recognize God, present in all things. To love God back. The wind of God, sweeping over the face of the water, to produce you. The Creative Word took on form, and substance, flesh for our knowing. God incarnate in all things, and in human being. The emphasis in "the Celtic tradition was that in the birth of a child God is giving birth to his image on earth."[65]

Celtic spirituality embraces the notion that this voice of God that calls all things into being is, in substance, God's own self, and therefore, God resides in all things. All creation is sacred because all creation is born of God. All creation is literally out of God's being. Newell tells us that John

Scotus Eriugena of the ninth century, a great teacher in the Celtic church, suggested, "If God were to stop speaking the whole created universe would cease to exist."[66]

There was a wind from God over the face of the water, again, when this Incarnate One whom we call Jesus stepped into the sacramental deep, when he went to his cousin John and got in the water of baptism. Witnesses said that when he came up out of the water the wind stirred, and there were rustlings all around, and such a wild beating of the air that the heavens were torn apart, and the Holy Spirit was visible in the wind. A flush, a flurry like flight. Like wings. Something that rides the wind, descending like a dove. God, with wings. Wind, with a voice. Words again. The voice with vowel sounds and consonants, "You are my Son, the Beloved; with you I am well pleased" (Mark 1:11). It was his anointing.

We anoint in baptism. A thumb of oil, and a cross on your brow, a holy glistening rubbed into your skin for your knowing that the Holy One inhabits human form. Your form. Oil on your forehead for your anointing, a sign in sacrament to mark, and remind you, that you are sacred, because the wind of God moved out over the face of the deep at your creation. To mark, and remind you, that you have been brought into being by God's voice, birthed by the word of God spoken, and that God is well pleased with you, and that you are God's holy habitation. You are not born of nothing; you are born of God. You are the dwelling place of God's Holy Spirit. You are the house, the temple. You are the tent. This holy pavilion for play.

The sky is changing. The temperature is dropping. A storm is brewing. The water of baptism is our bowl for playing creation as a ritual act. We gather at a font because God moves over the face of the water. The wind of God sweeps through, sails flap, sheets snap, it catches our breath, and lifts our spirits. We animate. And we are off on our high seas adventure of eyes opened to seeing God in all of the life we live, and naming God as the life, and spirit, in and all around us, like an epiphany, when we suddenly see what has been there all along. You are anointed in baptism. You are the beloved. God's Holy Spirit has torn open the heavens and has descended upon you. All around you, signs of the sacrament. With every breath that fills your lungs, with every creature that takes flight, you have been visited by the Holy One in wind.

God is made known to us in the song of a flute, the wind in a pipe. God is the whistling moan of a bamboo stand. Every swell of the great organ is a wind from God sweeping over the deep. Your own sweet voice, a sign. A sacrament in every sparrow, or leaf, or wisp of hair on your head as a way for you to see. A sign that God's Holy Spirit is ever in wind, and voice, and word to create you, and to bring you into being, and to give you life. God's long, slow work and steady art—and craft—of creation, and incarnation, has made its crescendo with you.

Initiative for Prayer

Prayer as Setting Sail with Baptism

Peregrine of the Celtic tradition would sometimes set a coracle, a very small boat covered on the underside with pitch, to the sea with no destination in mind, just to see where the wind of God would take them. The journey was worth the journey, simply to be out in it with God. Every soul on a journey with God is a pilgrim, even when the journey is simply coming and going from your front door. To enter into the experience of the Holy Spirit descending upon you as the wind that sets us on the adventure of pilgrimage with God, prepare one of these crafts. Ponder your life as a setting sail with the Holy Spirit, who descends upon and anoints us.

Make a sailboat out of any kind of floating container you might find around the house, or buy and build a model kit from a craft store. Now set sail. Find a city fountain, or small park pond, and set sail. Use a stick to guide your craft when it gets out of reach. Go to a park, or place where you can get your feet in the water, even if it's your bathtub, and blow your sailboat into action with the help of the straw from your oratory. On a large puddle set an upturned magnolia leaf, like a coracle, on the surface of the water. If the air doesn't stir the leaf after a time, breath out over the water. Ponder the power of the Holy Spirit in breath and wind. Ponder yourself on pilgrimage with God.

Our tent lifted, our pavilion launched with the wind, and we were off. We caught the wind for our play. Lifting our hearts. Soaring our spirits, raising our voices, heightening our imagination and inspiration. We caught the Holy Wind when the wind came to play.

Our stars still dangle from the mantle. Almost always moving, even if just a bit. The draft of an open door, or the fireplace heats the air and turns them around, a person walks by, and the air stirs our poster board stars, twisting and turning to be: God seen. For me. My heart lifts. God catches me up. And we are off on the high seas. "Hoist the sails." "Ahoy, matey." It's all play, these holy days and God's Holy Spirit.

Initiative for Prayer

Crafty Prayer, Monastic Prayer

I call this monastic prayer because as much as we imagine monks to sit silently in prayer and adoration, monks are in fact industrious and work with their hands. Remember that monks live in community. Think of the images of monks raising and tending sheep, and making cheese and wool. Remember monks keeping a garden, cooking for the refectory, and washing pots and pans. Remember nuns starting a school or tending the sick and caring for those wounded in battle. Remember the *Book of Kells* and the scribes working in the scriptorium on sacred manuscripts. I call this prayer initiative monastic prayer because you are making something. So, here's an invitation to using the crafty work of your hands as prayer.

Cut poster paper stars and moons, thread them with fishing twine or thread, and hang them overhead inside the tent, allowing the tent to serve as the dome. Allow your drawing, cutting, and threading of the stars and moons to be prayer. Meditate on God's delight in creation, the sky, the heavens, the dome, all for God's delight, and yours. Make up names for what you might call each star. Once you've suspended your stars and moons inside the tent, see God in the movement of air that makes them twirl or sway. Spend some time in this pavilion, and think of some names for God that you've never used before. Write a prayer using a new name as the address.

Prayer as Praise and Memorization

Get inside the tent each morning or evening, and read and recite portions of Psalm 104 until you have them memorized.

Bless the Lord, O my soul.

O Lord my God, you are very great.

You are clothed with honor and majesty,

wrapped in light as with a garment.

You stretch out the heavens like a tent,

you set the beams of your chambers on the waters,

you make the clouds your chariot,

you ride on the wings of the wind,

you make the winds your messengers,

fire and flame your ministers. . . .

By the streams the birds of the air have their habitation;

they sing among the branches. . . .

When you send forth your spirit, they are created;

And you renew the face of the ground.

I will sing to the Lord as long as I live;

I will sing praise to my God while I have being.

(Psalm 104:1–4, 12, 30, 33)

If you don't want the clutter of leaving your tent in place for a week, suspend the stars and moons from a doorway, or from the ceiling of an out-of-the-way corner, or even from the inside of an umbrella.

———————

14

LENTEN JESTER

On a frigid day in January, the sons of a Navy pilot gathered around a narrow shaft of frozen earth in our memorial garden. I crouched over the grave, to shift and pour the cremains of the brave old man into a drawstring shroud, a holy duffle of fair linen. The wind swept through, and God animated his body one more time as dancing ash. Up and all around in a twirl. His own glorious gesture of "Alleluia, alleluia, alleluia."[67]

We make our song at the grave. Our Easter song. Our simple tune of resurrection, the threefold Alleluia, because the Lord is risen, and so are we. We make our song at the grave. On Good Friday and Holy Saturday, we perch graveside and wait for the wind, whisper, and chant, and teeter at the edge. We keep vigil, for God to stir up the ash. Animate! Desperate for God to show, to sweep through with the holy wind, and breath of resurrection. For by then, after forty days and forty nights, and all the drama of Passion Week, we are worn and weary, and we have tasted death; we are ready with our Alleluias.

We get dangerously close to the grave on Ash Wednesday, but not just any grave. None other than our own. We reach into the soot of death, and smudge mortality at our crown. We let death touch us on the head. We look it square in the face: we are dust. Ash. Dirt. Humus. Decaying matter. Handfuls of earth. Human. Mortal. Subject to death and decay. And for that frightening glance, our liturgy tells us, remember. "Remember that you are dust, and to dust you shall return."[68]

Echo and reminiscence. A reminder filled with allusion to Genesis. Our liturgy tosses a gift our way for this risky Lenten journey. A sage reminder in the face of death, and the grave. Remember your creation, so that you can imagine your resurrection. Remember that you are dust, because "the Lord God formed man from the dust of the ground, and breathed into his nostrils the breath of life; and the man became a living being" (Genesis 2:7).

You are dust. A word that at once holds memory, and hope. Same dust. Same ash. Same dirt. Same God. Bending for handfuls of humus. Fistfuls of forest floor, gloriously fragrant with the rich decay of living matter. And God, fashioning and breathing again. As in creation, so in death, for resurrection.

Initiative for Prayer

A Garden Plot: Prayer as a Practice of Hope

Buy some flower bulbs. Daffodils, tulips, hyacinths. These are all "Easter" flowers. Symbols of something dead, such as a crusty old bulb, coming to new life. Dig as many pockets of earth as you have bulbs. Sit with the earth and imagine the open earth as a series of graves. Plant each bulb, plant it deep in the earth, and as you do, sing, or say the words: "Alleluia, Alleluia, Alleluia."

From time to time, sit at this garden spot. Contemplate your breathing. Whisper prayers. Sing the Alleluias. Light a candle and stay present as a vigil of resurrection. Say your name to God. Listen for God to say yours. Bring your journal along, and a pencil or crayons. Journal anything that might present itself to you. Or color an abstract of God scooping you from the earth, and breathing life into you. Look around you, and notice evidence of God's presence in the element of air. Watch for verification of wind, sound, scent. Visit this place in all kinds of weather.

Watch through winter, into early spring for the bulbs to sprout and flower. Allow yourself to live in the same hope, and expectation, that makes us sing at the grave. Depending on the climate, the planting activity may take place in late winter, rather than fall.

Prayer as an Act of Compunction:
A Weeklong Project

Study the Air Quality Index

Spend some time reading up on air quality, and what factors go into this scientific calculation. Keep a journal page for one week, recording the Air Quality Index for each day. When you record the day's index, jot down a thought or two about the Holy One in air. As you contemplate the Sacred Presence in air, ponder what it means to participate in the pollution of this sacred space. Allow yourself to consider your own responsibility taking for the care or neglect of the dome that separates the waters and animates all life. Write down some positive intentions for yourself.

A Threefold Confession

As you reflect on this during the week, fill in the blanks of the threefold confession, using three separate sheets of paper.

- I have been ...
- I have not been ...
- I have been ...
- I confess to you, O Holy One in air who animates.
- For my ...
- For my ...
- For my ...
- Accept my repentance, O Holy One, the breath of my being.
- Help me to ...
- Help me to ...
- Help me to ...
- Restore me, O Sacred Wind.

Act of Compunction

In a safe place, on a bare patch of earth or concrete, make a circle of stones to hold a small fire. Tear the sheets of your threefold confession into pieces. Place your confessions in the center. Light them with a match. Stir the papers with a stick until all parts have a chance to burn. Now stir the ashes themselves. Sit with the ashes until they are cool enough to dip your thumb into them for a smudge of ash.

Smudge the first mark, a cross or another mark of your choosing, at the top of your sternum. Say some words, such as those suggested above: I confess to you, O Holy One in air who animates.

Smudge the second mark, beneath the first mark. And say: Accept my repentance, O Holy One, the breath of my being.

Smudge the third mark, beneath the others, deep into the rib cage. And repeat again: Restore me, O Sacred Wind.

Absolution: Blessing Your Breathing Apparatus

With your thumb, join the three small marks together in one large, generous action, and say a prayer of thanksgiving and absolution. Make up your own, or try this one: "Thank you, O Sacred Breath, for restoring us, for giving us your mercy, and for the spirit of reconciliation, and amendment of life. Bless you for the cleansing wind with which you renew and forgive us. Amen."

When my Sally was three or four years old, she took on the role of the self-appointed household Lenten jester. She had been to our Mardi Gras parade, and she had helped us bury the Alleluia banner to silence our celebration for six long weeks of Lent. She knew, but she refused to put away her Alleluias. Out of the blue, in the background of every day, she continued to sing her Alleluias. Grinning, and laughing, and generally pleased with herself, defiant to church rule and Lenten discipline, she persisted, and without fail it made me laugh, or chase her around the house, or sweep her tiny self off her feet.

It made me laugh. Her audacity. Her bold-faced, gutsy proclamation of the gospel. This clever soul in miniature belting out with verve, our graveside song, our threefold Alleluia, or skipping them down the sidewalk, sometimes even wagging her tail with amusing antics designed to make her mother laugh. And finally, I got it.

Humor has to do with our capacity for the absurd, even "the ludicrous."[69] This is the absurdity of Easter faith, that God will raise us from the dead. It is laughable. The whole lot of us, laughing, and singing our Alleluias. And jumping around the house and skipping them down the sidewalk. As if we were four years old. How absurd. And so very funny.

All of us like blessed Thomas. Demanding, daring Thomas. The absurdity of his faith. He wanted to touch the body. Dubbed as the doubting one, but he was the very one who got it. Thomas saw his beloved Christ tortured, beaten, bruised, and bloodied. The body of his beloved with the life gone out. And if he had visited, if his beloved had visited, Thomas needed to touch him to know it. Thomas demanded a body, because there was a body in his death, and if there is no body in his resurrection, then there is, really, no resurrection.

We do some pretty silly things in the church, but this most of all, the most absurd of our faith: we stand at the grave and sing "Alleluia, alleluia, alleluia." God with breath, breathing again into dust, and ash, to animate, to give us voice, the verve and audacity it takes to sing our Easter song at the grave, and the breath it takes to make us laugh. Life out of dust and ash. How ludicrous. And deliriously thrilling.

———————

Initiative for Prayer

Laughter Yoga:
Practice the Joy of the Holy Spirit

I'm sure there are volumes written and YouTube demonstrations galore of laughter yoga. It's a real thing. Here's the disclaimer: I am not a yoga instructor, nor do I "practice" yoga. However, on occasion my husband and I will wing it with what we consider to be "laughter yoga," when one of us is struggling with darkness, or even just the blues, or winter doldrums.

This is how we do it: One of us invites the other to laugh, and then begins to "fake" a nice belly laugh, complete with such things as throwing one's head back, or whatever other natural gestures make sense for laughing. Then perhaps we vary the breath, and body posture, to mimic all sorts of ways of laughing, and the other joins. You can even pretend you're going to wet your pants if you don't stop. Eventually, you will both, or all, be genuinely laughing. There's an expression that says, "Laughter is the best medicine." Maybe this is because laughter is an experience of Holy Spirit and the Holy Spirit is Healer.

Prayer as Pilgrimage and Play:
Field Trip to a Cemetery

Since a cemetery is a holy site, it's especially appropriate to call this a pilgrimage. Consider the theological reality that we find God in the elements, in particular today, in air, and how air is experienced in breathing. Pack a basket to include lunch, a blanket, writing materials, bottles of bubbles, a kite or two. Include some family or friends on this trip, to increase the frivolity. Consider, and anticipate, the breath of God.

Spread the blanket and lie down in quiet on your backs. Watch your belly, and chest cavity, rise and fall with your breathing. Consider the gasp of the newborn, and the gasp of the resurrected. Blow bubbles as an experience of holy play. Consider the round, floating bubbles of life. Chase them. Catch them. Blow them above your head, and let them fall on you, or watch them catch the Holy Breeze, and get carried away, high into the sky. Look at them from a distance, and revel in your ability to see the Holy Spirit move across the cemetery. Breath, visible in the air, because of the bubbles. If the wind is right, and this is not a cemetery with lots of trees, try flying some kites to catch the wind. As the kite lifts and sails, contemplate the notion that you are seeing the animation of the Holy Spirit. Write some thoughts, or a prayer, or a poem, in your journal. Or draw a picture of the kite in the sky. Add a fanciful tail to the drawing.

15

DANCING AROUND THE GRAVE

Roadkill. Cat's rat. A dog with a bone. There are a million ways to die. And I have died at least a thousand deaths. I have buried myself in the grave and made choices that caused my decease. Choices that keep me dead. Choices that keep me wondering whether or not I exist. Choices that confirm that I am no matter.

I have counted my own bones. I have chewed on cinders. On this side of the grave, I have borrowed from death with a backhoe and truckload of burying; my life slipping into the grave. An avalanche for stepping too close to the pit. Can these bones live? Tell them Ezekiel. Tell the bones. Tell them about the breath (Ezekiel 37). I'm just wild about Ezekiel. Scandalous, and raw, and I'm crazy for him. Sifting, and sorting, in a valley of dry bones. I'm right there with him. He roots around in my stomping grounds.

Jesus tantalizes me in the story about his dead friend Lazarus, by asking Mary and Martha, "Where have you laid him?" Jesus is like me—he wants to see the dead body. And then, he says, "Take away the stone." And then, "Lazarus, come out" (John 11).

I am wide-eyed. My want, for bones to live. My bones. Yours. A bodily resurrection. Nicene. Apostles. Athanasian. The Creeds. And I cross myself when I say "I believe in . . . the resurrection of the body."[70]

I believe in the resurrection of the body because I want it. I want the body. God in the body. Mother in the body. Life and love in the body. I want to feast again, and dance, and love, and laugh, and sing, and rest, and play, free of death. In the body. To live. Again.

I have danced around the grave enough that I have tripped my way to the other side, and I have decided to borrow, instead, from Resurrection. My beloved, my incarnate Christ, my Benno, plays a tin whistle, and he dances on the grave, and sings there, and the breath of God that is in him, makes me live, too. The wind for the dry bones. Tell them, Ezekiel; tell them about the breath. He whistles in a tin flute, and it makes me dance. Holy Spirit in wind, the air in the flute, and in the breath.

I have been raised from the dead. But since I've died a thousand deaths, it will take a thousand resurrections. Christ descended to the dead and has burst my prison. I have already begun the kingdom life. I can sing, and dance, and feast, and borrow days from heaven, because there are enough days to lend, because it is just that—life, everlasting.

Initiative for Prayer

Prayer as Wordless Breath and Vibration

Consider the simple possibility that prayer can be wordless because air and the Holy Spirit can provide utterance too deep for words. Two possibilities for wordless prayer are sounds caused by vibration and rhythm. Music.

Buy a tin whistle, or a kazoo if you're a little shy about experimenting with music, and go to a field, or an underpass in the city, or any place outside and away from judgmental listeners. Play a tune. Just keep playing until you get a sense of what sounds you like. Then offer them to God. Listen to them and see if you hear the Holy Spirit in breath, and rhythm, and wind, and vibration, coming to you, out of you.

Another option is to buy or borrow a drum.* Again, go to a place where you can be free of listening judgment. Play a bunch of different rhythms. Try using your hands rather than sticks or implements. Get into it. Let your body flex and move. Rest a moment and do it again. Try a different pace, a different combination; use one hand instead of two. See if you can feel the vibrations on your chest, in your body, and your heart, depending on how you hold the drum. Ask the God of air, of holy vibration, of rhythm, and beat, and ancient of days, to heal you.

---

*Crafting tip: If you cannot arrange to borrow or buy a drum, an excellent choice is to crisscross wide packing tape on one end of an oatmeal box or #10 tin can.

He brought me out by the spirit of the Lord and set me down in the middle of a valley; it was full of bones. (Ezekiel 37:1)

He cried out with a loud voice, "Lazarus, come out!" The dead man came out, his hands and feet bound with strips of cloth, and his face wrapped . . . (John 11:43–44)

We get it: death is serious business and we're headed straight for it.

You have to love Ezekiel. A graphic, passionate, priest and prophet. He delivers God's word to Israel in little one-act plays, and poems, and riddles, and shocking visions. Anything to get their attention, to get them to see, and hear, the impending doom and devastation that awaits. And so, he did things. Dramatic, scandalous things, at God's instruction.

King Nebuchadnezzar was advancing toward Jerusalem, so Ezekiel was to enact a siege by hemming himself in with bricks of the kind they had in Babylon, and then he was to eat unclean food, and rationed amounts of grain and water. The Lord told him he was to bake his barley-cake in the sight of the people on a fire built of human dung. But even for Ezekiel, that was just too much. So, they negotiated, and the Lord gave in, and said, "See, I will let you have cow's dung instead of human dung, on which you may prepare your bread," but weigh, measure, and ration, and show the people what life is like under siege (Ezekiel 4). On another day, he shaved his head and beard with a sword to demonstrate their impending military defeat, that they would be prisoners of war. Shaven. Hairless. Bald. Another time, he built a stage with a wall, and packed up his belongings, and dug through his wall, and climbed through carrying his bags, as they would soon do themselves on their way to Babylon. Their walls would be broken down, and they would carry the luggage of exiles.

Great stuff for third-grade Sunday school stories.

But the most poignant of all, Ezekiel's wife, his delight, would die. And God forbade him to grieve. "Yet you shall not mourn or weep, nor shall your tears run down. Sigh, but not aloud; make no mourning for the dead" (Ezekiel 24:16–17). And when he did it, the people were aghast. "Why are you acting this way?" He likened it to their attitude about the near and certain loss of their precious sanctuary. It would be profaned and they wouldn't grieve, because they didn't care.

For all his wild-eyed carrying on about indictment, and disaster, doom and destruction, when the day came, and Nebuchadnezzar set the siege, and laid waste to Jerusalem? Ezekiel was right there with them, a priest and prophet to his people on the forced march into exile. And there, as a captive in Babylon, he started up again. Words, and oracles, and poems, and visions, and dramatizations, but this time, about hope. Return and restoration. A lunatic for love. You have to love Ezekiel.

Ezekiel brings God to us in one of the most provocative intimate prophecies I think I've ever read in Holy Scripture. He says, for God, "I am going to open your graves" (Ezekiel 37:12). And I feel myself gasping big and scrambling to hold them shut. Right there like Martha and Mary, stiff armed to hold him back, panicked about the decay in there, inside the grave. All my graves. All your graves. Places where you've buried your dead. All the quiet moments, and hidden places, where we've died a thousand deaths. Carefully wrapped worm-eaten flesh; and God says: I'm going in.

Private places, secret griefs, the proverbial skeletons in the closet. Sacred taboos about the dead and keeping secrets. Silence, and soft voices, stepping over and around the gravesites. Rules so we don't defile our burial grounds, but God says, "I am going to open your graves."

Ezekiel, in his wild-eyed visionary self gets a walkthrough of the mass grave of humanity. The valley of dry bones. And Ezekiel said: "It was full of bones . . . and there were very many . . . and they were very dry (Ezekiel 37:1–2). No soft tissue, no spongy substance inside. Dry. Hollow. Rattling bones. No more life-producing, re-creating system for the human body. Dry. Empty. Rattling bones. The marrow gone out. No new blood, no red cells or white. No platelets. No stem cells to craft another generation. No protection or immunities. No transplants. No donors. Exponential death. A valley of dry bones. Ezekiel down in the middle of the valley, and it was full of bones, and they were very dry.

And God commands Ezekiel, "Prophesy." Tell the bones about the breath (Ezekiel 37:4). And Ezekiel tells the bones about the breath, and God moves out over the valley with his breath.

God hovering. Bones rattling and shaking at the nearness of God, the heat of divine breath; hot breath with moisture. Holy Wind sweeping, rushing, roaring over dry bones to breathe life, like the Holy Wind at the creation of the world. God in creation bringing all things into being. God speaks, breathes, stretches out over worm-eaten flesh and hollow bone, and makes it live. This is Resurrection: "I am going to open your graves . . . [and] when I open your graves . . . you shall live" (Ezekiel 37:12–14).

Bone, then sinew, and flesh, and skin, and Holy Wind. The Breath of God. Life out of the grave. Creation, all over again, but resurrection this time because it is life—out of death.

In a New Testament rendition of the story, Jesus said to Martha, "Where you have laid him?" (John 11:34). It seems he glances my way, and yours, with a want to know where we have buried our dead. What of ourselves have we wrapped and tucked away in the hollow of a cave? What of us has already begun its decay, and its return to the earth? For Ezekiel's people, it was heart and home. Spiritual, emotional, physical exile. Exponential death. Prisoners. Powerless. And far from home. Is that where we are?

Or perhaps we keep company with Martha and Mary. Standing there in the abandonment of being left alone while Jesus makes us wait—the sufferable absence of God, the intolerable waiting on the Son of God. Broken, and bitter, while we ready the grave, and do our digging.

It all mirrors back to us with a tug. Where have we done our dying? Where have we done our digging of the grave? No matter that it's been four days and already brewing a stench. God is going in.

Ezekiel, tell me about the breath. The Holy Breath that goes out over the valley of dry bones, and gathers me, and finds all my missing parts, femur and phalanges, skull, jawbone, ribcage, and hip. God collects, and reconnects, and fashions me again, and then . . . the breath. And I can move. And sing, and skip, and dance. And live and love again. In the body. "I am going to open your graves . . . and you shall live" (Ezekiel 37:12–14).

Initiative for Prayer

A Project as Prayer in Two Parts

Consider the question Jesus poses to Martha and Mary about Lazarus: "Where have you laid him?" He asked them where they had laid their dead.

Part One: Inventory Project

Set aside thirty minutes to reflect on your life in broad strokes. Your history: events, decisions, relationships, and timelines. Your internal life: thoughts, dreams, goals, and hopes. The changes over time in your heart, soul, mind and strength, as a person. Use your journal to scribble a few thoughts, or track them as you might a timeline. See if you can think of three (choosing a random number here) moments or ways when you have died, so to speak. Write them down on something such as cardboard, a smooth stone, or paper, and wrap each with strips of cloth. Paper towels can work just as nicely. Now, choose three different places to "bury" or hide these. Outside or inside. Be creative if you like, about where things can be hidden or tucked away. Or take a classic route, and get a trowel, and head outdoors to dig a little hole for each. Pause with the exercise—for three days.

Part Two: Guided Meditation Based on John 11

Imagine Jesus coming down the road toward your place, and go out to meet him on his way. Tell Jesus any objections you might have on the tip of your tongue, as Mary and Martha both did, when you see him. Just let it rip. Now imagine Jesus asking you, and listen carefully for his voice: "Show me where you have laid him."

Take Jesus to each of your three burial sites. Show him where you put them, and how you buried them. Hear him say your name, followed by the words, "Come out," and the words, "Unbind them and let them go." Then, do it. Open the grave, the burial site, the stack of things, the place where you have hidden these. Do the unbinding, or unwrapping, and letting go. Welcome back this life of yours. How is it different without the death? Without the sorrow? How does it feel to let it go? How does it feel to unbind, and be unbound? Use your journal, if you wish, as it might take a little processing, and perhaps over time.

Initiative for Prayer

Prayer as Field Trip: Prayer on the Hoof

Visit a cemetery. Take your journal or some paper and pencil. Or use the notepad on your smart phone. Wander around through the head stones. Make a list of the names that you see. Make your prayer a Resurrection Roll Call. Start by calling out, "Everybody up." Call out the list of names. Say them out loud. Try singing some of them. Try the singsong voice of childhood when you called someone home for dinner, and they were in the far reaches of the neighborhood. Call out your own name. Welcome your own self. Open your arms in greeting. God tells Ezekiel: "I am going to open your graves . . . and you shall live" (Ezekiel 37:12–14). Call out loud to yourself, these words that God said to Ezekiel.

Journal exercise: Consider any, some, or all of these reflection questions: How does God call you to life? To live? To be alive? What are the dry bones in your life? Can they live? What happens inside of you when you hear the words: "I am going to open your graves, and you shall live"?

16

FLYING FEATHERS

Over coffee and a mid-morning dessert of berries and chocolate, Liz, a woman friend who, like me, shares the romance of fly fishing with her beloved, slid a newspaper clipping from the *New York Times* across the counter. The headline: "When Fashion Meets Fishing, the Feathers Fly."[71]

Apparently, there's a shortage of feathers. Apparently, feathers are just like hair, and they are "cutting-edge chic . . . they can be washed, blow-dried, curled and flat ironed and they don't fade." The article went on to say, "Dry flies typically use brown and neutral feathers, which some women prefer for a more natural look, and flies that sink often use feathers in colors like yellow and electric blue, which deliver more pop as a hair accessory. Feathers that used to cost a few dollars each are fetching $20 in some salons." A sixty-five-year-old fly fisherman from Maine said, "It's sacrilegious." According to the article, fly-fishing feathers individually are called "hackles," and as a group are called "saddles." Don't you love those words? Feathers. Hackles. Saddles. Plume. Quill. Pinions. Flying feathers.

In a Hebrew poem, numbered 91 among the Psalms, God has feathers. God is a winged being. "He will cover you with his pinions, and under his wings you will find refuge; his faithfulness is a shield and buckler." God with wings. God a nesting bird. God hovering. God bearing, God bearing down, and birthing, God bearing up, and rescuing. God with a brood.

There are names for God that roll easily off the tongue, such as Father, or Lord, and maybe Shepherd. But God is also rock, and fortress; a mighty outstretched arm; and God is warrior, and Holy Comforter. God is ox, and God is eagle. God is lion, and lamb, servant king, and suffering servant. God is light, and fire, and water. And air. And God is a winged being.

The psalmist tucks us in, defended by the fierceness of a mother bird whose very bone and feather are shield and buckler. Maybe we find those wings suffocating and overwhelming, to have God that close. God so close that we are intoxicated by the scent of comfort and battered by the beating heart of this flying feathered winged being. Maybe we don't like that.

At the end of his life, Moses sings God, with wings.

> As an eagle stirs up its nest,
> and hovers over its young;
> as it spreads its wings, takes them up,
> and bears them aloft on its pinions,
> the Lord alone guided him;
> no foreign god was with him.
> He set him upon the heights of the land,
> and fed him with produce of the field;
> he nursed him with honey from the crags,
> with oil from flinty rock . . . (Deuteronomy 32:11–13)

Maybe we are uncomfortable with the God Moses knew. The God known for the speed, and power, of her wings, the wings with which we are rescued, delivered, snatched out of slavery. Saved. Or maybe we are the Jerusalem Jesus loved and lamented. "How often I have desired to gather your children together as a hen gathers her brood under her wings, and you were not willing!" (Matthew 23:37). Maybe we don't like that mothering.

Or perhaps we just don't know the position of squatting under those wings. The clinging atop those soaring wings. Perhaps we might enjoy the love, and favor, of the divine wings, the safety, and intimacy, the refuge, and peace, the heights, and habitation, the joy, and feasting pleasures of the brood, the honey from rock. Perhaps we just don't know.

In prayer, and spiritual imagination, I do my work of grinding stone, and re-imaging God as winged being, this Mother God who would hover and feed, bear me up and tuck me under. Your spiritual work may not involve the grinding of stone. Your work may be but an endearing: a joyous celebration, a minor forgiveness, an internal inventory, or a mission of mercy. I don't assume for one minute to fill in the blanks. I do assume that you have images of God. They are yours to keep, to enjoy; to grieve, to shed; to inhabit, to embrace. To uncover our images of God is for our wholeness, and sometimes, for our healing.

Initiative for Prayer

Body Prayer and Positioning

Take different positions for prayer; try a variety of postures. Stay in each position for the timing of a minute, eventually you might want to keep the position for a longer period of time to experience more or different manifestations of God. Think about, or write about this in your journal, as your experience of God, or language of prayer, or just scribble a bit about your musings, or sketch yourself.

1. Try squatting down under God's wing, like a bird with a brood. Add a sheet or blanket draped over you for effect, if it helps. In the quiet, what do you hear? What do you feel? What do you know about God from this position?

2. Try lying down on your stomach, on a surface that has an edge to it, perhaps a table or a bed. Take hold at the edge with both hands, like you are on eagle wings, being carried aloft. What do you feel, what do you see?

3. Curl up in a feather bed or duvet. Meditate on God as a nesting bird with feathers to make a nest. Meditate on the image of yourself in the nest.

Along the road where I run when I'm in Pennsylvania, I pass by the edge of a picturesque sheep-grazing farm, which, compliments of the dawn-to-dusk cutting of bulldozers and back hoes, has become a construction site for "Chamberlain Ridge Estates." I don't recall ever seeing sandpipers around my home. But there they were. Shorebirds looking for the sea where the sea wasn't. Sandpipers running stiff-legged along the stripped dry dirt, as if a wave might just roll in anytime now, and we lived a seven-hour drive from the Jersey Shore.

Suddenly, in an epiphany-like moment, I could see myself in those birds. Day after day I wrote about my life in my journal. Volumes. They became my constant companions, and mental company, that summer. I wrote reflections on my childhood, my career, my former marriage. Sandpipers separated from the sea. No wind. No wave. No tide, high or low. Far from the sea and stranded. I had already considered how dangerous it would be for them to make the journey back to the sea.

Unfortunately, the day before I left Pennsylvania, I had to bury one of the sandpipers. It was flattened on the road, and by the time I made it back with my shovel it was nearly one with the pavement. But still, I wanted them to go. Take flight. The small speckled shore birds on parched land made me want them to take the risk, to ride the wind. To fly.

In Psalm 91, we find ourselves whispering to a God with wings. Before we know it, the psalmist lures us into the dark shadowy refuge, and seduces us to worship a God with wings. You are "my refuge and my fortress; my God, in whom I trust" (Psalm 91:2).

Our words slip out, and position us underneath divine feathers; the long flying feathers of the sacred one. "He will cover you with his pinions, and under his wings you will find refuge; his faithfulness is a shield and buckler" (Psalm 91:4). The psalmist postures us squatting under God's *kanaph*. The wing. The sweeping, spreading, skirting gesture, of God's presence.

Moses sets us on the soaring, lofting, lifting, flight of God, with eagle wings, as an eagle who bears us up on its pinions and sets us atop the heights. God with flying feathers. God, in the wind.

Initiative for Prayer

Prayer as Awe and Wonder; Prayer as Research

Use Google, or get out a good old-fashioned encyclopedia, and study up a little bit on air currents. Log some of your findings in your journal. How are they different in different geographical settings, for example: what are the air currents for seabirds at the sea, or for eagles among cliffs or mountains? How is it that birds fly, or ride the wind? What are some bird wing shapes? You might want to sketch some of the patterns of air movement in your journal, along with some sketches of the landscapes and habitats where different birds are found. Try your hand at an Audubon sketch of the bird wings.

Prayer as Storytelling and Retelling

On a journal page: try writing or rewriting a prayer, using bird wing, and wind, language. Just write, don't evaluate or craft what you are writing. Make a list of ten prayer starters, with wind, and wing, and bird language for the name of God. You can keep it simple, and all the same, just start each line with "O . . ." and fill in the blank. If you are feeling inspired, add a phrase to one or two of the "O Names" before moving on. Then, move in with an ask. Choose one. What would you ask of this particular image of God?

Then, think it over, consider the writing experiment: What resonated with you? Where did you experience resistance? What new thoughts or images came to mind, and delighted you, or confused, or surprised you?

A parishioner texted me late in the afternoon, apologizing for having involved me in one of her missions. We had had lunch together that day. We got out of her car near the *Taquiera de Sol* and headed down the sidewalk past some shops, and we heard, or rather, she heard, some frantic chirping, and immediately stopped to investigate. The sound drew us to two enormous planters big enough to house tall prickly cedar trees, the planter's round ledge rising above my knees. And the tree, well, it was super tall. Up high, we saw not one, but two nests. Both empty, save for the baby bird on the top nest who made all the clatter. It looked as though it was perched on the edge of the nest, and lost its balance, clinging on but head-down in a nosedive, wings flapping for dear life.

After considerable debate and a search for mother bird, we decided, at my suggestion, to go eat lunch; and if when we returned, the situation was the same, I promised we would do something. So naturally, forty-five minutes later, Gini was hoisting me up, barefoot, onto the ledge of the planter, shoving me into the prickles so I wouldn't fall out as I stretched, both arms to my farthest reach to tuck the bird back into the nest. But lo and behold, the bird's leg was in a tangle of fiber-like vine, a piece of the nest twisted around, dangling the bird like a snare.

I cupped the bird. My heart raced at the sensation of a wild creature's beating heart and flapping wing in my hand. A delicate grasp with one hand, the other to untwist the twine around its now useless leg, and with a flurry and flush of feathers it was gone in a flash. It flew for its life. A fledgling's first flight, never to return to its nest of captivity. Like two crazed women we darted around the parking lot saving it again, and again, scooping it up from sizzling pavement to the shade, lifting it out from parked car windshield wipers to pine straw under a holly hedge.

It could fly. It had a bum leg, but it could hop, and it could still fly. I was exhilarated. Full of inspiration about my own life. My life, Gini's life, your life. So, when she texted me that afternoon, I texted her back, "No apologies," and added, "I love knowing that I touched feathers that still fly."

It was a thrill. The most ordinary common sparrow had become sacrament. An everyday every-moment sacrament, an outward and visible sign of inward and spiritual truth. Every bird a kind of knowing the unknowable, seeing the invisible: God's Body, wing. God's Spirit, wind. And not only "listening for the heartbeat of God"[72] but feeling it thump in my hands.

As my friend Liz and I mused over the *New York Times* clipping about feathers flying when fashion and fishing meet, I thought to myself, and said in an almost giddy whisper, "I have feathers that still fly."

My beloved and I planned to go fly fishing at dawn, and later that day I would don a bit of vintage linen, and lace, on the banks of the Rogue River. And I would tuck some feathers in my hair, and in with a fistful of herbs and wildflowers to carry, as sacrament. In every feather a testament that God's Spirit is wind; God's Body, wing. Feathers in hand as a celebration in sacrament, that I have taken to the wind, and made my journey back to the sea.

Initiative for Prayer

Portable Oratory

For your portable oratory, add feathers. Add a straw. You might find feathers as you walk about if you look at the ground, or buy some at a fly-fishing store or craft store. The former will more than likely offer real feathers; the latter may sell man-made materials; either is fine. (See "A How-to for the Oratory and the Prayer Journal" on page 6 for further instruction.)

Process Prayer: Observation, Reflection, Meditation

Go to a fly-fishing store, which is often called a fish hawk. Wander about among the feathers for sale. Touch them. Pick them up. Jot down some of the names of the different feathers. When you have a chance to sit down with your journal:

1. Consider the differences in feathers, and how they might be used by the bird for flying, or nesting, or strutting about. Compare the strength, length, and size, softness, fluffy quality, or rigidity, straight, curly, colorful, patterned, or whatever variations you observe.

2. How is God present to you in these thoughts? How do the variations in feathers help you understand God?

3. Meditate on God with wings, and God, riding the wind.

Prayer as Watchfulness

Go bird watching. You can watch birds out your window, from your porch, sitting at a sidewalk café. Or go for a walk in a city park, a woodland walkway, a conservatory, or Audubon lands. Use binoculars or your naked eye. What is the dynamic between wind and wing, and the bird's body with the air? Just watch, and wonder, and seek to understand and experience God.

Prayer as Costuming

Collect or buy some feathers that suit your fancy. Be brave and creative. Tuck some in your hair. Make some earrings. Glue some on a headband or tie clip. Attach them to a hat. Sew some along the hem of a garment, or string them as a necklace. Wear feathers as a sacrament that shows you with a sign and symbol on the outside what is true on the inside: God's Body, wing, God's Spirit, wind, residing in your soul, and you, "listening for God at the heart of life."[73]

NOTES

1 *The Book of Common Prayer and Administration of the Sacraments and other Rites and Ceremonies of the Church: Together with the Psalter or Psalms of David. According to the Use of the Episcopal Church* (New York: Seabury Press, 1979), 861.

2 *The Book of Common Prayer,* 88.

3 J. Philip Newell, *Listening for the Heartbeat of God* (New York: Paulist Press, 1997), 1–2.

4 *The Book of Common Prayer,* 861.

5 *The Book of Common Prayer,* 861.

6 Esther de Waal, *The Celtic Way of Prayer* (New York: Doubleday, 1997), 140.

7 *The Hymnal 1982 according to the use of The Episcopal Church* (New York: Church Publishing Incorporated, 1985), 370.

8 *The Book of Common Prayer,* 305.

9 *The Book of Common Prayer,* 376.

10 De Waal, *The Celtic Way of Prayer,* 145.

11 J. Philip Newell, *Christ of the Celts* (San Francisco: Jossey-Bass, 2008), 39.

12 *Merriam-Webster's New Collegiate Dictionary,* 9th ed. (1991), s.v. "deplete."

13 *The Book of Common Prayer,* 358.

14 *The Book of Common Prayer,* 378.

15 Newell, *Listening for the Heartbeat of God,* xvii.

16 *The Book of Common Prayer,* 376.

17 De Waal, *The Celtic Way of Prayer,* 70.

18 Newell, *Listening for the Heartbeat of God,* 35.

19 De Waal, *The Celtic Way of Prayer,* 35.

20 De Waal, *The Celtic Way of Prayer,* 47, 93.

21 De Waal, *The Celtic Way of Prayer,* 92.

22 *The Book of Common Prayer,* 124.

23 *The Book of Common Prayer,* 124.

24 *The Book of Common Prayer,* 123.

25 De Waal, *The Celtic Way of Prayer,* 58–59, 61.

26 *The Book of Common Prayer,* 378.

27 *The Book of Common Prayer,* 287.

28 De Waal, *The Celtic Way of Prayer,* 17.

29 *The Book of Common Prayer,* 861.

30 *The Book of Common Prayer,* 211–12.

31 J. Philip Newell, *The Book of Creation* (New York: Paulist Press, 1999), 12.

32 *The Book of Common Prayer,* 211.

33 *The Hymnal 1982,* 65.

34 The Iona Community, *Iona Abbey Worship Book* (Glasgow: Wild Goose Publications, 2017), 106.

35 Newell, *Listening for the Heartbeat of God,* 35.

36 *The Hymnal 1982,* 112.

37 *The Book of Common Prayer,* 118.

38 *The Book of Common Prayer,* 118.

39 *The Book of Common Prayer,* 308.

40 Newell, *Christ of the Celts,* 36.

41 Newell, *The Book of Creation,* xviii.

42 *The Book of Common Prayer,* 285.

43 *The Book of Common Prayer,* 285.

44 Newell, *The Book of Creation,* 37–38.

45 *The Hymnal 1982,* 423.

46 Newell, *The Book of Creation,* 19.

47 Newell, *The Book of Creation,* 19.

48 *The Book of Common Prayer,* 306.

49 *The Book of Common Prayer,* 306.

50 *The Book of Common Prayer,* 306.

51 *The Book of Common Prayer,* 149.

52 *The Book of Common Prayer,* 281.

53 *The Book of Common Prayer,* 306.

54 Newell, *The Book of Creation,* xii.

55 Newell, *The Book of Creation,* xxiv.

56 *The Book of Common Prayer,* 311.

57 *The Hymnal 1982,* 83.

58 J. Philip Newell, *The Rebirthing of God: Christianity's Struggle for New Beginnings* (Woodstock, VT: Skylight Paths Publishing, 2014), 90.

59 Newell, *The Book of Creation,* 103.

60 Newell, *The Book of Creation,* 19.

61 Newell, *The Book of Creation,* 20.

62 Newell, *The Book of Creation,* 20.

63 Newell, *The Book of Creation,* 20.

64 *Merriam-Webster's New Collegiate Dictionary,* s.v. "elixer."

65 Newell, *Listening for the Heartbeat of God,* 14.

66 Newell, *Listening for the Heartbeat of God,* 35.

67 *The Book of Common Prayer,* 499.

68 *The Book of Common Prayer,* 265.

69 *Merriam-Webster's New Collegiate Dictionary,* s.v. "humor."

70 *The Book of Common Prayer,* 496.

71 Katie Zezima, "When Fashion Meets Fishing, the Feathers Fly," *New York Times,* sec. A1, June 29, 2011.

72 Newell, *Listening for the Heartbeat of God,* 1.

73 Newell, *Listening for the Heartbeat of God,* 1.

Printed in the USA
CPSIA information can be obtained
at www.ICGtesting.com
JSHW012052140824
68134JS00035B/3390